The odds Are In Your Favor—

Sound nutrition for your baby begins *before* he is born—as a matter of fact, before conception!

A mother-to-be who prepares her body for its task by raising it to the highest level of health gives her baby the best chance for a healthy birth and life, while benefitting herself at the same time.

In this uncomplicated, pleasant program based on natural foods, Gena Larson shows you how to ensure your baby's nutrition from the pre-conception period to kindergarten years— and how to help yourself and your family to a longer life of "feeling better."

Gena Larson's

FACT/BOOK
ON
Better Food
for
Better Babies
and *Their Families*

Keats Publishing, Inc.　　　　New Canaan, Connecticut

Gena Larson's
FACT/BOOK on Better Food For Better Babies and Their Families

Pivot Original Health Edition published 1972

Copyright © 1972 by Gena Larson

All Rights Reserved

Library of Congress Catalogue Number: 72-83519

Printed in the United States of America

PIVOT ORIGINAL HEALTH BOOKS are published by
Keats Publishing, Inc.,
212 Elm Street, New Canaan, Connecticut 06840

To Bonnie and Donna, my beloved daughters-in-law, who have given me six precious grandchildren and a great deal of help with this book.

Preface

This book has been prepared with sincere respect for the parents or prospective parents who have a deep reverence for life. Who believe that the body is indeed the "temple" of the spirit and who seek to preserve and maintain that "temple" through intelligent care of their minds and bodies. To such parents will be born children with a proud genetic inheritance, infants who need no mending.

The recipes included in this book stress the use of whole, natural foods, used raw or lightly cooked.

Many foods can be prepared by blending, chopping or jelling, instead of by cooking which results in the loss of vital nutrients.

Most foods suggested in the recipes for children would be entirely suitable for the older members of the family, with the addition of a bit more sophisticated seasoning, just as food prepared for the family table can be adapted to meals for the infant and toddler.

It is hoped that the recipes will be of help to you in creating nutritious new foods or in adapting family favorites to more healthful methods of preparation.

The health and well-being of your family and, in turn, the community and world of which they are a part, will depend largely upon the food prepared for them each day.

Let us seek for the knowledge and information to make creative nutrition and delicious natural foods part of our children's daily living experience. If we fail in this, whatever else we do will be of little importance. With this knowledge we can create a new generation, with better babies, happy families and a better world for all.

Introduction

Each year the number of babies born with physical or mental defects increases. Newspaper headlines proclaim the tragic figures; magazine articles tell how to care for these pitiful little ones, in the home or institution; special classes are set up to help them learn; plastic surgons repair destorted or unfinished bodies; but alas, very little, if any, time or energy is spent in teaching our young people how to have healthy, normal children.

Young people have a right to know that the kind of food they eat, from birth until they become parents, will affect the physical and mental health of their children. Nutrition and other measures to build abundant health, should be taken before pregnancy, not during pregnancy only, for a child will inherit the quality of health that his parents have been preparing for him for a lifetme.

G.L.

Contents

PART ONE

PRE-NATAL AND PRE-SCHOOL NUTRITION

Chapter I

Pre-Conception Diet and Suggestions

BASIC NEEDS

Perhaps the two most critical years in a child's life are the two years before he is born. During the year previous to conception, both parents are building the specific health (or lack of health) into their bodies that will provide the genetic inheritance of their child.

Since our genetic makeup remains the same for every human being, our basic needs are just what they have been for centuries.

1. Pure, nutritionally sound food, grown on highly mineralized soil, poison-free and eaten raw or lightly cooked.
2. Fresh, pure air and gentle sunlight.
3. Pure water to drink.
4. Exercise, appropriate to the age and individual.
5. Sleep, rest, and repose.

Parents, planning their first child or even to improve the quality of life inherited by subsequent children, must first of all insure that these basic needs are met. The body will then build the good genes that will result in a child with a normal, healthy body and mind.

The exception to this would be where one or both parents are the bearers of defective genes inherited from their parents or grandparents, so defective that normal genetic inheritance for their child is impossible, in which case adoption may be considered.

If a child is well nourished from the year before conception with natural foods, pure water and fresh air, he will be much better able to provide a superb genetic inheritance for *his* child.

Primitive people, in every part of the earth, knew exactly how to preserve their tribal patterns of health, vitality and beautiful, perfect bodies and to pass this gift of radiant life down to their children through countless generations.

Dr. Weston Price's book, "Nutrition and Physical Degeneration," is one of the most exciting works on this subject. Even a child will quickly get the idea that the diets of natural foods, native to the specific areas, resulted in the birth of beautiful, healthy babies, while the eating by the parents, of the processed "foods of convenience" resulted in sickly, mis-shapen and defective bodies. The fine photographs are self-explanatory and the well-documented dietary records and histories are unforgettable. This book is available from the Price-Pottinger Foundation, 2901 Wilshire Blvd., Suite 345, Santa Monica, California 90403. Many public libraries have it also.

Since our goal must be to give every child born a body free of inborn illness and imperfections, with built-in resistance to disease and premature aging, let us learn and do the things that will bring an end to this tragedy that the late Dr. Royal Lee has called "Unfitting the Unborn."

We must be concerned with raising the quality of life in each child, giving to each precious little one his full share of abundant health.

PREPARATION FOR DIET: DAILY REQUIREMENTS

Preparation for conception might well begin with some type of inner body cleansing. Many doctors advise a three-day juice diet or a mono-diet of good natural food to help clear out some of the toxins that most of us have accumulated over the years and give our digestive organs a rest: Three days of carrot and celery or zucchini juice, or of eating all the apples you wish, or the grape diet, both friut and juice; or juicy, ripe watermelons if they are in season. Chew a few seeds also or blend the watermelon seeds in apple juice, strain and drink that. Papaya or grapefruit will also be very effective—any fresh ripe fruit in season. Drink pure water in between your meals of fruit or juice.

Consider the use of a concentrated acidophilus culture from your health food store for at least a three-month period after the initial cleansing, to re-establish the friendly bacteria in the mouth, throat and intestinal tract. One-fourth cup of the liquid acidophilus mixed with 2 oz. of apple or pineapple juice taken shortly before mealtime, at least twice a day, will restore that wonderful feeling of well-being and help to bring the body to a state of radiant health. Or stir the acidophilus into buttermilk or yogurt and drink.

After the cleansing, begin your pre-conception diet. Foods of particular value at this time include:

1. *Life bearing seeds and nuts.* Sesame, pumpkin and sunflower seeds are delicious in fruit or vegetable salads. Sprouted seeds such as alfalfa, mung bean or lentils have increased nutrients. Try to include at least a cup of sprouted seeds in your menus each day. Use them in salads, added at the last moment to soups or stews or as the "greens" in sandwiches. They may also be enjoyed in lightly stir-fried Oriental type dishes.

Save and use all *seeds* from red and green sweet Bell peppers. Blend them into salad dressings for added flavor or sprinkle over salads or into soups and stews at serving time. Extra seeds may be dried or frozen in small packets for later use.

Seeds from cantaloupes, crenshaws, honey-dew or watermelon should be saved and utilized in a delicious Melon Seed Drink—see page 47. Melon seeds may also be juiced a few at a time, with apples or carrots.

Pumpkin seeds and the seeds from all kinds of

squash, including butternut and older zucchini, can be used in the Melon Seed Drink, above, juiced with apples or carrots or lightly toasted in the oven for a flavorful Squash or Pumpkin Seed Snack. See page 64.

Nuts may be finely ground into nut butters or soaked overnight in milk or pineapple juice for greater digestibility. To preserve freshness, keep cold while soaking. Drain and keep the resulting "fat" nuts in a covered jar in the refrigerator until used. The soaking liquid may be used to drink or in preparing other dishes.

Potatoes, sweet potatoes and jerusalem artichokes are also foods that bear life within themselves and all the vital forces to nourish the young plant. The "eye" or "germ" carries the valuable life source and every effort should be made to include these vegetables in our menu in the raw, unpeeled state to protect this precious nutrient.

Do *not* eat the *sprouts* of potatoes as these tubers are a member of the deadly nightshade family and the sprouts are highly toxic.

2. *Fertile eggs* from chickens raised on the ground and fed greens as part of their daily fare. Such eggs contain valuable hormone materials useful for maintaining endocrine gland balance. Fish roe is also in this category.

3. *Organ meats such as heart, brains, sweetbreads,* etc., but excluding liver, *unless* you are sure of the source.

4. *High quality grains,* soaked or sprouted or freshly ground, then soaked overnight and eaten raw or lightly cooked next morning. To eat raw you may like to soak them in juice or cream. Use water to soak if they are to be warmed. Whole grains may be soaked overnight in twice as much water as grains, then gently steamed for a bread replacement in some meals.

5. *Fresh raw vegetable and fruit juices.* These may be used in abundance. Sip ten minutes before each meal, and if desired, at bedtime.

6. *Fresh raw fruits*—two servings each day. Use a variety in season.

7. *Lactic acid foods* such as homemade yogurt, sauer-

kraut, beet borscht, sour-dough bread—also raw buttermilk, bleu cheese or Roquefort cheese. One or more of these foods could be served each day.

8. Some source of *raw protein* should be included in your meals every day, as well as the so-called "complete proteins," ordinarily served cooked. Remember, heat destroys part of many amino-acids, thus distorting the amino-acid pattern and making most cooked proteins incomplete. Examples of delicious raw proteins: egg-nog made from certified raw milk and fertile eggs, some cheeses, homemade cottage cheese, nuts, seeds, avocados and grains, soaked or sprouted.

9. *All sweets*—even good natural sweets such as dates, honey, figs, molasses and sorghum—should be used in *moderation*.

10. *Raw butter, raw cream* or *raw salad oil* should be used daily, 1 or 2 teaspoons. *Raw avocado,* bone marrow or sweetbreads are also good food sources for these vital "lipids." These are fat soluble nutrients that protect our very chromosomes, the little bundles of blueprints in our cells which are necessary for passing on the characteristics of the race.

Avoid all foods contaminated by synthetic chemicals and toxic sprays. Do not use "convenience foods," fabricated foods, or any food from which valuable edible parts have been removed or non-nutritive substances added. Examples: imitation ice milk, margarine, fabricated fruit drinks, white sugar, white flour, hydrogenated fats.

Grow some of your own foods if possible. At least grow sprouted seeds and grains in your own kitchen and parsley and mint on your window sill.

Search out sources of natural foods, organically grown, poison free. Try to find fruits and vegetables that have been ripened on the tree or vine for added nutrients.

Learn to enjoy from sixty to eighty percent of your food raw. This will cut your food bill down, perhaps thrity percent, as at least one-third of the nutrients in cooked foods are destoryed by heat.

Especially try to eat something raw at the beginning of each meal—fresh raw vegetable or fruit juices, raw vegetable appetizers, salad first, soup later—at home or even eating out.

Many times you can serve a large green salad plus another raw vegetable such as sliced tomatoes, avocado, celery sticks, or a raw fruit to begin or end the meal.

Eat a wide variety of foods in season, especially in your own area, but do include also natural foods in season from other areas too. Pecans from Texas or Utah, avocados from California, papayas from Mexico or Hawaii, etc. will furnish different trace minerals from the soil in these areas and add interest to your menus.

Foods held in storage lose nutrients. Out of season, choose sun-dried fruits or freeze, dry or can your own vegetables and fruits. There will be loss of nutrients in homecanning but you will know the food was poison-free and without additives.

In cooking, use the lowest possible temperature for as little time as possible. Use tight stainless steel, glass or ceramic utensils with tight, partially vacuum-sealing lids, and little or no added liquid. Keep and use every drop of the cooking liquid.

SAMPLE MENUS

A simple diet pattern follows. (Recipes for starred items will be found in Part Two of this book.)

SAMPLE MENU NO. 1.

Upon Arising:
> 1 teaspoon codliver oil (cold pressed) free of pre-servatives, followed by warm water with 1 tablespoon lemon juice or cider vinegar.
>
> *Breakfast:* Fresh raw fruit in season such as strawberries or apples and bananas. Top with yogurt (made from raw milk or cream, if possible.) Sprinkle with 2 tablespoons raw wheat germ or sesame seeds or freshly ground nuts.

Lunch: 6 to 8 oz. fresh raw vegetable or fruit juice. After 10 minutes, large raw vegetable salad including sprouts and greens. Add some sort of raw protein to the salad: seeds or nuts, grated cheese (swiss or cheddar), cottage cheese or avocado. Top with your own mayonnaise* or yogurt dressing.* If no protein in the salad, you may serve lightly cooked fresh fish or eggs. To drink: buttermilk or kefir. Herb teas may be served here or in between meals. Take supplements now. (See end of chapter).

Dinner: 4 to 6 oz. raw vegetable juice. Example: tomato or carrot and celery. Small to medium green salad or cole slaw made with added alfalfa or bean sprouts. 1 teaspoon wheat germ oil can be included in the salad dressing. Lightly cooked green or yellow vegetable. Baked or steamed potato or sweet potato or squash or brown rice.

Buttermilk or kefir or herb tea now or later. Food supplements.

Fruit for dessert, or later in the evening, if you wish. Drink water between meals for better digestion.

It is good to have the day's complete proteins early, at breakfast and lunch, when the body enzymes will have a better chance to completely digest them. If this is not possible, because of working away from home, have an adequate lunch and a small serving of protein at the dinner meal.

SAMPLE MENU NO. 2.

Upon Arising:
1 teaspoon codliver oil followed by warm water with lemon or cider vinegar. You may wish to exercise before breakfast.

Breakfast: Super Cereal;* freshly ground grains; seeds and nuts, several kinds, soaked overnight in milk or apple juice served with yogurt, sliced fresh fruit in season, two or more kinds and served with honey or molasses.

—or—

8 ounces eggnog* from fertile eggs, raw certified milk, carob or vanilla to flavor, very little honey or molasses to sweeten; plus a dish of fresh peaches or apricots.

Lunch: To be taken to work or school—6 oz. carrot-celery juice in thermos. Fresh vegetable sticks, peppers, carrot, cauliflower, etc. Open face sprouted grain bread sandwich with butter oil spread,* alfalfa sprouts and lettuce and a slice of cheese or meat for the top.

—or—

Tuna fish salad* in jar, raw buttermilk or kefir to drink. *Fruit,* fresh and raw, for dessert or at "coffee break" time.

Dinner: 6 oz. carrot-celery juice or 4 oz. fresh apple juice. Green leafy vegetable salad, Roquefort dressing, raw beet relish. Vegetable-meat soup, corn tortillas with butter, herb tea to drink, now or later.

Before bed: fresh raw fruit and milk or buttermilk.

Supplements you may wish to take to further safeguard and improve your health:

1. Vitamin E, for both prospective parents, from 200 to 400 International Units each day, *1 teaspoon wheat germ oil* (use in salad dressing or take from a spoon) and *1 tablespoon fresh raw wheat germ* on cereal or salad. These are all part of the same food complex and are most effective when used together.

2. Vitamin C, from 500 milligrams upward. To normalize the metabolism, protect from virus and infection and to help combat allergies and promote antibody formation. Use a food source of bioflavinoids in addition, such as the white part of the skin of oranges or grapefruits or red or green sweet bell peppers.

3. A balanced natural vitamin-mineral supplement,

preferably one made from the juice of cereal grasses or other plants, with the moisture removed, and which contains large amounts of unknown nutritional factors as well as all known nutrients. Your health food stores will have several good brands. Sources from which you can obtain natural supplements by mail are listed at the end of this book.

Use generous amounts of this supplement to insure adequate nutrition at this very important time, since any excess will be harmlessly discarded by the body and too small an amount will result in a waste of your investment.

4. A balanced B complex, 1 or 2 each day, especially if noise, smog, tension or stress are unavoidably present in your life pattern.

5. Blackstrap molasses, 1 or 2 tablespoons each day, as an extra source of organic minerals and trace minerals. Use on cereal or rice or in boiling water as a beverage.

In addition, avoid the use of any known harmful substance such as alcohol, tea, coffee and tobacco. Use no sleeping pills, aspirin or tranquilizers. Many doctors now recommend that the prospective mother avoid any medication at all for at least twelve days prior to the onset of menstruation as it is during the first ten days of life that the embryo is most susceptible to insult and alteration from drugs. Often the woman may not know she is pregnant for at least thirty days; therefore there is no alternative but to avoid the use of drugs as completely as possible at this time.

Chapter II

Pre-Natal Diet And Suggestions

After conception, the mother's body alone supplies the nutrients to the child, but the prospective father still has many essential parts to play in this drama of the beginning of life. He will, of course, continue to support his wife in her objective of providing the growing fetus with every needed nutrient each day and to provide an atmosphere of joy and love in which this can best be accomplished. In addition, he will wish to make their home as safe as possible and to protect his wife from every possibility of accident or trauma.

A daily walking program can be a time of relaxation for both parents. Plan to spend weekends or vacations in areas where the air is pure and there are many trees. He will also wish to help his wife to find time for adequate sleep and rest.

At the beginning of pregnancy many women find that five or six small meals a day are easier to digest than three larger meals. Just be sure that the six small meals contain all the essential nutrients and are not just "snack" meals.

Extra tablets of B^6 and B^1, or foods rich in these vitamins, used daily, will many times prevent "morning sickness." Foods rich in these B vitamins are brewer's yeast, wheat germ, bananas, sprouted mung beans and lentils or fresh raw pecans.

There should be very little difficulty with "morning sickness" or other unpleasantness if the body cleansing and other healthful practices have been established for a year or so before conception. Discuss this with your doctor. Many times he will suggest keeping a piece of whole wheat toast by the bedside and eating this slowly before getting up.

Many doctors now feel that restricting the weight gain of a pregnant woman to only 10 to 14 pounds may be a contributing factor in our country's high infant mortality rate and, particularly for the fifteen- to eighteen-year-old mothers, increases the biological risk a great deal.

A pregnant teenager, who is still growing, will need a great deal more protein than an adult woman. Dr. Janet C. King of the University of California at Berkeley, did a recent study of the metabolism of ten girls aged fifteen to nineteen during the last three months of their pregnancy. She found that their bodies could use almost *four* times the amount of protein formerly thought adequate. Mothers-to-be of this age might well consider a powdered protein supplement to be used once a day, in juice or milk, from the third to the sixth month and twice each day thereafter. Several good brands will be available at your health food store or order by mail from sources listed at the end of this book. Try to find one with a complete amino acid pattern, made from uncooked proteins. Soy milk powder or brewer's yeast may be added to the daily egg nog for extra protein, if no powdered protein is available.

Tom Brewer, a medical doctor practicing in the San Francisco area, tells us that even doctors are sometimes misinformed about the vital importance of a good, well balanced diet in pregnancy. Some doctors even put their patients on a starvation diet. Dr. Brewer advises the mother-to-be as follows: "Don't go on a starvation diet. If you gain a few extra pounds during pregnancy from eating a good, well balanced diet, it won't hurt you or the baby, even if you gain 50 or 60 pounds. Worry if you don't gain enough weight." He goes on to say: "You may be given 'diet pills' to take away your appetite—! Don't take them! You may be given diuretics or 'water pills' during your pregnancy—Don't take them!

These drugs are not needed to have a healthy pregnancy and a healthy baby." [1]

The ideal diet would, therefore, be one which included every essential nutrient, every single day—not one particularly low in calories. It is better to have small regular meals every day, than to feast one day then eat less for several days to make up for it. Some of the baby's cells and organs are being formed every day and good nutrition is important to the health of those cells and organs. Remember, it is not healthy for either you or your unborn child to go without good food even for twenty-four hours.

SAMPLE EATING PATTERNS

1. *Upon arising:* Glass of warm water with juice of ½ lemon or 1 teaspoon cider vinegar.

    Breakfast: 6 oz. fresh orange juice or ½ grapefruit or 1 sliced orange. 2 tablespoons raw soaked grain cereal with any fresh fruit in season and yogurt or cream. Flavor with honey or molasses. Whole or sprouted grain toast, if desired. Take food supplements.

    Mid-meal: Apple slices with almond butter (or fresh almonds soaked overnight in juice or milk) or glass of certified raw milk or buttermilk.

    Lunch: 4 to 6 oz. carrot juice with a little beet juice or the juice of greens. 1 coddled egg on whole wheat toast with 1 teaspoon raw butter spread.* Take supplements. Nap and relax.

    Mid-meal: Tossed green salad with cottage cheese in the dressing, or 6 oz. green drink* with sunflower seeds.

[1] Dr. Tom Brewer. "Pregnant and Want Your Child" 1969, Berkeley, California (ed.), Nutrition Action Group, 3414 22nd Street, San Francisco, California 94110

Dinner: 4 to 6 oz. fresh carrot juice. Small dinner salad or cole slaw. 4 oz. broiled fresh salt water fish with yogurt-dill sauce.* Steamed greens (turnip, mustard, kale, etc.). Cup of yogurt or buttermilk with added acidophilus concentrate—1 to 2 tablespoons. Take supplements.

Before bed: Fresh raw fruit in season and/or milk or buttermilk.

2. *Upon arising;* 1 glass of warm water or juice with acidophilus concentrate.

Breakfast: Sprouted grain bread, lightly warmed or toasted with butter oil spread,* mixed nut butter,* orange marmalade* raw. Hot herb tea or molasses drink. Take supplements.

Mid-meal: Banana eggnog.*

Lunch: 4 to 6 oz. fresh raw carrot, celery, beet juice. Raw green salad with alfalfa sprouts and ½ an avocado diced. Sprinkle generously with grated raw cheddar cheese; serve with yogurt dressing.* Milk or buttermilk. Take supplements. Nap and relax.

Mid-meal: Green drink* with sesame seed.

Dinner: 4 to 6 oz. carrot and greens juice. Carrot-pineapple salad with honey yogurt dressing.* Baked potato with yogurt or butter oil spread.* Hot herb tea with honey or hot molasses beverage. Take supplements.

Before bed: Fresh raw fruit or cup of yogurt.

3. *Upon arising:* 1 glass warm water with juice of ½ a lemon or 1 teaspoon cider vinegar.

30 minutes later: Apple juice (raw) with 2 tablespoons acidophilus concentrate. Supercereal* with dates and ½ ripe banana sliced, yogurt or cream. Hot herb tea or molasses beverage if desired, or milk. Take supplements.

Mid-meal: Boysenberry-kefir drink. Or eggnog.

Lunch: 4 to 6 oz. carrot-celery juice. Green

salad with mung bean sprouts, tomato, French dressing. Broiled fresh fish with butter oil spread and chopped fresh dill. Take supplements. Nap and relax.

Mid-meal: Sliced fresh pear with bleu cheese. Glass raw certified milk or buttermilk.

Dinner: 4 to 6 oz. carrot and greens juice. Sliced tomatoes, onion slice. 2 corn tortillas or homemade cornbread* with mashed avocado. Hot herb tea with honey or hot molasses and water beverage.* Take supplements.

Before bedtime: Fresh raw fruit. Glass buttermilk or stewed prunes with yogurt.

4. *Upon arising:* Glass of warm water with juice of ½ a lemon or 1 teaspoon cider vinegar.

30 minutes later: 3 oz. fresh grape juice (raw) with 2 tablespoons acidophilus concentrate added.

Breakfast: Flaxseed cereal* with dates and pecans. Serve with raw cream or nut milk or apple juice. Take supplements.

Mid-meal: Dish of yogurt with honey or fruit purée over it. (Raw apricot or peach purée is good.) Or eggnog.

Lunch: 4 to 6 oz. carrot and beet juice. Celery stuffed with peanut or almond butter. Homemade vegetable soup with diced avocado. Sprouted grain bread with raw butter spread. Herb tea, supplements. Nap and relax.

Mid-meal: Dish of berries or fruit in season with honey and raw milk and cream or nut milk.

Dinner: 4 to 6 oz. carrot and greens juice. Green salad with ¼ avocado diced. Hot buttered brown rice with soy sauce and freshly ground sesame seed. Buttermilk or raw milk to drink. Take supplements.

Before bedtime: Fresh raw fruit in season with yogurt.

If you have no vegetable juicer and there is no health food store near you from which you can purchase your raw juices, just do the best you can.

If you have a blender, carrots may be finely ground in apple juice or raw milk and used in place of carrot juice. Liquid salad or green drinks may be made in your blender. You will find recipes and directions for these in the recipe section of this book. High quality green herbs and vegetables are very important in your diet and should be used generously.

Try to include every day of every week:
1. Four glasses of milk (raw certified, if possible). Whole, skim, buttermilk or kefir are some of the kinds you may choose.
2. Two eggs—at least one of them raw.
3. One or more servings of fish, chicken, organ meats, lamb, or other meat, or cheese. Any kind or two kinds of raw seeds and nuts.
4. One or two servings of fresh, green leafy vegetables, some of them raw. Mustard, kale, broccoli, collards, chard, dandelion, lettuce.
5. Two slices of whole grain bread.
6. One serving of citrus fruit or melon or a glass of fresh orange or grapefruit juice—*not* canned, bottled or frozen, except in case of an emergency—plus one or two servings of any other fresh fruit you enjoy such as: bananas, apples, peaches, pears, apricots or plums.
7. One serving of whole grain cereal such as oatmeal, cornmeal or "granola." Fresh raw wheat germ may be added at serving time for extra flavor and protein.
8. Try to have 1 cup of sprouts every day. They are easy to make, easy on your budget and delicious! In addition include in your diet:
   a. A yellow or orange colored vegetable five times a week at least; yams, squash, carrots, rutabagas, etc.
   b. A whole baked potato, including the skin,

three times a week. A piece of raw potato
may be eaten in addition. Try it grated into
your salad or into vegetable soup just at
serving time.

c. 1 teaspoon or more butter or butter oil
spread.

d. A moderate amount of salt each day. Sea
salt has more available minerals than ordin-
ary salt. If it is available, by all means use it.
Kelp powder, which has a slightly salty taste,
may be used in addition if desired.

Daily doses of vitamin B⁶ appear useful for easing
nausea in the last trimester of pregnancy, as well as
easing other disturbances such as swelling of hands and
feet, pain in finger joints and muscle spasms.

Ask your doctor about the use of a vitamin K supplement in your eighth month.

Fresh raw seeds and nuts are a fine snack or mid-
meal food and can be enjoyed by themselves or with
fresh fruit. Even though there is an increased need for
high quality protein during pregnancy, of even more importance is the need for perfect digestion and assimila-
tion of the protein consumed. Some mothers find protein easier to digest in the earlier hours of the day. If
you do, omit the complicated proteins from your evening meal and before-bedtime snack. The easily digested yogurt or buttermilk can usually be taken with the
later meals with no ill effects.

Raspberry leaf tea has been found most helpful to the
mother-to-be. Our grandmothers knew this and modern
research is reaffirming the truth of this folklore. Use as
a beverage between meals or after meals—the recipe is
on page 65.

During the latter months, because of pressure on the
vital systems, some expectant mothers are troubled with
constipation. To help overcome this, several natural
methods may be used.

1. 1 teaspoon "Chia seeds" may be soaked overnight in one-half glass of water, then taken first

thing in the morning, adding both bulk and a lubricant to the bowel.

2. A serving of soaked or puréed prunes may be eaten at bedtime, topped with ½ cup yogurt.

3. Ground flaxseed may be sprinkled over your breakfast cereal or fruit, or the flaxseed cereal—see page 67—may be used at breakfast or suppertime.

4. 1 tablespoon brewer's yeast may be used daily in juice or mixed with peanut butter.

5. Raw okra, in season, may be sliced and used in salad or added to soups or stews at the time of serving.

6. Raw wheat germ added to your breakfast cereal or fruit salads is sometimes of help.

TELEVISION VIEWING

The expectant mother should limit her television viewing to a very few hours a day. It is best to sit well back from the set; this will help to protect her from the dangers of television radiation. She should be especially careful about turning the set on or off. Stand to one side. There is growing evidence that long hours of television viewing by the mother may result in the child being particularly susceptible to leukemia.

Recent research has shown vitamin C gives good protection against ionizing radiation from whatever source. In addition to your daily supplement of this vitamin, try to include at least three foods high in vitamin C in your food intake each day. Cabbage, red or green sweet peppers, broccoli, parsley and other raw green leafy vegetables are reliable sources of vitamin C when organically grown, and used as soon after picking as possible. Bananas, apples, fresh pineapple, papaya, watermelon and cantaloupe—as well as the more familiar citrus fruits—all carry important stores of vitamin C as well as many other vitamins and minerals.

Sprouted seeds are another valuable source of vitamin C. (Catharyn Elwood's book, *Feel Like a Million,* now available in paperback, is one of the finest books to teach the sprouting of seeds as well as other aspects of nutrition.) Sprouts may sometimes be purchased at your health food store or from your nearest oriental market.

The use of pectin daily will help remove strontium 90 from the blood by way of the digestive tract. Since all milk, even mother's milk, contains this dangerous element, it would be wise to begin use early in pregnancy to prevent storage in the body and later, through the milk, in the infant.

Two organically grown apples each day will supply the needed pectin. If they are not eaten, take powdered pectin, with no preservative, in one-half glass water or juice.

Sunflower seeds are said to be helpful also. They may be added to your salad or eaten as a snack.

SMOKING

Women who smoke during pregnancy are particularly vulnerable to illness and infection. This is particularly true for the teenage mother-to-be as the additional nutrient demands of pregnancy may compromise their growth potential and increase their risk in pregnancy.

Women who smoke deliver infants of significantly lower birth weights and the more they smoke the lower the birth weight of their babies. These infants may be harmed permanently because of the adverse effect of the deficient nutrition during the last three months of pregnancy. Dr. John Dobbing of the University of Manchester, England, has found that the most important formative time for the brain is just before and just after birth. If the child does not get proper nourishment then, he may have permanent mental disability. Smoking may dull the appetite so proper food is not eaten at this critical time. Smoking also destroys vitamin C in the body.

Chapter III

Baby's First Years

NURSING YOUR BABY

The one best food for baby is mother's milk. Mother's milk is more easily digested and always available at the proper temperature. Night feedings are easier for the new mother—no waiting to heat a cold bottle while the baby cries with hunger. Travel is safer for the breast-fed baby—no danger of a change in formula.

Nursing is certainly the most economical way to feed your baby. You might like to add up, sometime, the cost of feeding a prepared baby formula and baby food for six months. Enough to pay for household help for the new mother, or to take the whole family on a three-weeks' vacation? Yes, indeed!

Another advantage in nursing your baby is time saved each day. No sterilizing of bottles. No preparing and warming formulas. Just your own high quality milk, formulated especially for your own little one. Always ready. Always the correct temperature. This is a real blessing in the first few weeks after the two of you return home from the hospital. You will need time to regain your strength and to get acquainted with your precious child.

Once you have decided upon nursing your baby, tell your doctor upon the *first* visit. If you find he is not the least bit enthusiastic about your decision, find out why. There will still be time to shop around for another doctor who will support your efforts in this vital function. If your doctor is encouraging but not too knowledgeable about nursing, continue with your plans to nurse and educate *him* as you study and learn about it.

Sometimes well meaning friends or relatives will try to discourage a young mother from nursing her child. This is a time when the husband can lend moral support and encouragement and say to all: "We have decided that our child is going to be nursed!"

For the mother, breast-feeding may help prevent cancer. Statistics show that women who nurse their babies are far less likely to get breast cancer.

Another result of nursing your baby can be seen for at least thirty years. One can examine the stool of any person, up to the age of thirty years, and tell by the presence or absence of certain essential bacteria whether or not that person was nursed as a child.

Before birth the placenta provides antibodies against a variety of infectious conditions. Breast-feeding promotes this process and should be continued for at least six months, after which the infant starts to manufacture his own antibodies. The well-nourished mother will have milk that is entirely adequate to sustain a high degree of health in the child.

One month before the birth of your baby, begin bathing the breasts, particularly the nipples, with a mild solution of sea salt and water. (¼ teaspoon to one cup water.) This will strengthen them for nursing.

The *ONLY* time it may not be wise to nurse is when a child is born with a serious illness, such as leukemia, heart or brain malfunction. Then it may be better not to nurse as the defective gene (or diet) that produced the defective child may hamper milk quality and production.

If the baby cannot be nursed, find a safe source of certified raw goat's milk or cow's milk. Dilute with bottled water in the amount specified by your doctor and add blackstrap molasses in a proper amount to regulate the baby's bowels. A tiny bit of brewer's yeast may be added for extra nutrients.

When safe raw milks are not available or the baby

cannot tolerate them, for various reasons, some other way to nourish the baby must be found. Some infants thrive on the raw seed or nut milks,* mixed as above with safe water, molasses and brewer's yeast. Other babies do well on a lightly cooked vegetable broth made from zucchini, carrots and parsley. This is strained into fresh raw carrot juice and diluted with water. Mashed avocado, diluted with mineral-rich water* has also been used successfully by some mothers.

If pasteurized milk is all that is available, try to get the product "Eugalan," a cultured powder made from mothers' milk. This contains millions of the friendly 'lactobacillus bifidus' which aid in digesting and assimilating pasteurized milk. Look for it in your health food store or order by mail from the source listed at the back of this book. The powder is easily mixed by pouring 4 oz. of lukewarm water into a jar. Add 3 measuring spoons of the powder, cap the jar and shake. The resulting liquid can be kept in the refrigerator. Add 1 teaspoonful or more to each bottle of milk you prepare for your baby. Your doctor will help you decide how much water, molasses, brewer's yeast and other supplements if any, to add to the bottle also.

If baby must be fed from a bottle, hold him in your arms while he is eating. Yes, I know you are busy; but you need a moment to rest and relax, and your baby needs most urgently the contact of your warm and loving arms to let him know he is safe with you and that you love him.

La Leche League, a nursing mothers organization whose whole sole purpose is to aid nursing mothers and all mothers everywhere, will be happy to offer helpful advice and suggestions. To learn more of La Leche League, write to 9616 Minneapolis Ave., Franklin Park, Illinois 60131, for brochures and information on the group nearest you. Or call your local childbirth education society. Mothercraft classes are sometimes taught at the YWCA, and the teachers will know of local La Leche Leagues. Look for their very fine book—*The Womanly Art of Breastfeeding*—at your local library or bookstore. It can also be ordered by mail from La Leche League, address above.

How Long to Nurse: One week is better than none. One month is better than one week. Three months is still better. Ideally, the infant thrives best if nursed from one year to eighteen months, or even two years if possible.

If the little one is completely breastfed, with no solids or supplements before the age of six months, the well nourished mother will have an ample milk supply.

One wise doctor in our town tells anxious young mothers who are asking about supplementary foods for their babies, "Fine, fine—whatever you think he needs, *you* take it and he will get it."

Adequate sleep as well as good nutrition is necessary for the manufacture of vitamin B in your body. This controls milk production. Do not be too quick to supplement if your milk supply lessens temporarily. Listening to your hungry baby cry is the most effective milk production stimulant known.

The child who is *not* nursed may need a natural vitamin-mineral supplement. Try to find one prepared from organically grown cereal grass juices or other plants.

When mother is ill (unless the illness has directly involved the mammary glands), do not deprive your baby of the antibodies in your milk at a time when he needs them most. He will be exposed to air-born bacteria and virus in the air, not from your milk. You can wear a mask while you are nursing if you wish.

When to Nurse: Nurse the young infant when he cries to be fed and *only* when he cries to be fed. Between meals he should sleep or play as long as he wishes. Let him take as much milk as he wants but do not urge him to take one more swallow than he wants. If the mother's supply of milk is ample, the baby should be able to drink his fill in ten to twenty minutes. This type of demand feeding is based upon the belief that a normal healthy child will take enough food to supply his own nutritional needs. Life for both the mother and baby is more comfortable than with a rigid schedule. Mother is able to provide comfort whenever the child cries and he soon learns that he is in the hands of someone who loves him.

One young woman, wise in the art of "mothering," told me that when she takes her baby up for his feeding at night or in the early morning hours, she places in the baby's bed a heating pad turned on medium heat. After the leisurely feeding, she removes the pad and places him back in a warm and cosy bed.

Take It Easy: When you feed the baby, put your feet up and relax. Some mothers, especially for the first few weeks, will enjoy lying down to nurse the little one.

Take a nap each afternoon when the baby naps. Try to rest *before* you get tired.

If possible, hire a helper. If you can't, get your relatives to help. They will be anxious to get acquainted with the new baby anyway. Try to drink lots of liquids and eat many good fresh foods each day.

Don't try to reduce at this time, for if you have gained a few pounds they will gradually slip away as the months go by.

Cuddle your baby. Love and enjoy him. Housework will wait but babies grow up faster than you would ever believe.

So many young mothers have told me that the use of brewer's yeast in their diet has helped them to produce an ample quantity of high quality milk, that I must mention it here. Adelle Davis gives detailed instructions for the use of this and other supplements in her fine book, "Let's Have Healthy Children" now off the press in a revised form. Many libraries have a copy that you may borrow.

MINOR ILLNESSES

Any new food in the mother's diet should be taken in moderation at first. If some food eaten by the mother gives the baby a loose bowel, one teaspoon scraped raw apple may be fed him. Carob powder is helpful also. One teaspoonful may be mixed with ¼ cup warm water and ¼ teaspoon raw honey and fed in a bottle, or from a spoon. Acidophilus concentrate (1 teaspoonful) added to water or juice, is often of benefit. This concentrate may be found in your health food store. If the diarrhea is severe, stop all food but the acidophilus and water and call your doctor at once.

If a mild sore throat develops in mother or baby, raw pineapple juice, (1 to 3 tablespoonsful) taken every hour during waking hours will often digest the troublesome virus and eliminate the need for harmful drugs or antibiotics.

It is important to know that the chief cause of infant indigestion is toxic bile from the liver of the child. During the first three years of life, this green-colored bile is thrown into the baby's bowel for elimination. Even mother's milk may form rubbery curds at such times. When this occurs limit the baby's food to mineral-rich water (recipe on page 45) or to fruit and vegetable juices greatly diluted with the mineral water. Continue for as long as necessary for the baby's comfort. If using cow's or goat's milk, dilute with half mineral water for a day or two. Of course, if the parents are in radiant health at the time of conception, the child will not be born with a load of toxins in the liver and gas and indigestion in the baby—and worry and loss of sleep for the mother—will be avoided.

Colic: New findings indicate that most colic may be avoided if the feet of the tiny baby are kept warm and comfortable. The many nerve endings in the bottom of the infant's feet are very sensitive to changes in temperature. Warm booties, soft warm socks, or an extra little blanket will keep the child's feet warm and colic at a minimum.

Constipation: Babies who are nursed will rarely be troubled with constipation but if this should occur (or if the child is not being nursed), Dr. Kurt Donsbach has this suggestion: "Equal parts butter and raw honey or safflower oil and honey is a fine natural laxative for the infant. One half to one teaspoonful as needed. This tastes good, has no irritants and causes no griping."

BABY'S FIRST FOODS

Minimum equipment: A stainless steel food grater, cheesecloth or nylon net and a food grinder. A blender and a juicer will be very helpful also.

From two to four months, your nursing infant will need little, if any, other food. If you wish, you may offer him mineral-rich water in a bottle from time to time, but don't expect him to be very excited about anything in a bottle. If you can obtain organically grown oranges, you may offer him the strained juice (about ¼ teaspoon) from the tip of a teaspoon or mixed with water in a bottle, at about four months. If safe oranges are not available, sweet red peppers may be chopped and soaked, and the baby fed a tiny bit of the soaking water, strained.

Sometime between four and six months, you may wish to add codliver oil to your baby's diet: ¼ teaspoon to begin, gradually increasing the amount to ½ teaspoonful by the time the infant is about eight months old.

If your child indicates that he is beginning to need additional food (by a suddenly increased demand for nursing that continues for several days) it is time to introduce him to solid food. Usually this occurs between five and six months of age.

For the first few weeks, offer the new food midway between nursings, or after nursing, before he gets too hungry to be in the mood for something new. When a new food has been introduced, do not start another in less than five days. In this way, if the baby develops a sore bottom or other indications that he is not handling that particular food well, you can feed less or eliminate it for two or three days. Once a food has been started, however, it should not be omitted from the diet for any length of time, but a small portion fed at least once or twice a week; otherwise, it is possible for him to have an allergic reaction to his food when it is offered later.

The first feedings of solid food are usually easier if you hold your little one on your lap, in much the same familiar nursing position. If you let his head tilt back a little as you introduce each new spoonful, the food will go in with little difficulty. Start with ¼ to ½ teaspoon of any new food, increasing gradually as he becomes used to it.

Juices from organically grown fruits and vegetables are good first foods. Grate them fine and squeeze the juice through cheesecloth or nylon net. If you have a juicer or can obtain organically grown juices from your health food store, that is fine, too. Start with one to three teaspoons daily, of any one kind. Apple or carrot are good starters. Dilute with safe water or the mineral-rich water. Feed at room temperature from the tip of a teaspoon or from a bottle.

Mashed ripe banana may be offered at this time. Please *do not* purchase canned banana for your little one. Why should you buy an inferior food for over a dollar a pound when you can prepare in an instant a quality food for a few cents? *All* commercial baby foods should be avoided. Most contain harmful chemicals and far too much salt and sugar to be considered good foods. Thin the mashed fruit with mineral-rich water or certified raw goat or cow's milk.

As the weeks pass by and baby's appetite increases and his digestive system develops and is ready for increased solid foods, give him the good natural foods that nature intended children to have. Ripe papaya and peaches, pears, and nectarines are spoon ready. Just mash, dilute with mineral-rich water and serve. As your infant grows, use less and less water to dilute his food. Avocados are usually relished at the first taste, and your good homemade yogurt can be offered now.

Try scraped raw apple or beets; sieved cottage cheese will be enjoyed. Mashed ripe persimmons in season, or mashed dates are good foods that require a minimum of preparation. Potatoes and sweet potatoes may be grated and the juice pressed through cheesecloth or nylon net; add to carrot or apple juice for a better flavor. Berries may be blended and strained or mashed with water and pressed through a sieve for a delicious juice. Raw peas or green beans may be blended or chopped, soaked in a small amount of water, then strained. Raw almond butter may be offered at about ten months; dilute at first with mineral-rich water. Acidophilus concentrate may be added to this or any seed or nut milk made for baby.

After the little one is eating a variety of solid foods, one or two of them can be spoon fed each day, but some of the others—such as mashed avocado or steamed, puréed vegetables—may well be thinned with mineral-rich water and fed from a bottle with a cross-cut nipple. Various supplementary foods can also be added to these feedings such as a bit of brewer's yeast, bone meal, or molasses.

Sometime after nine months, you may wish to offer your baby milk to drink from a cup once or twice a day. Try to find a safe raw certified milk or goat milk for him. If that is not possible, get the best milk you can and add to each cup 2 teaspoonsful of "Eugalan," cultured from mother's milk, and available at health food stores.

Dissolve the day's supply of the powder, 6 to 8 teaspoons, in 4 ounces of lukewarm water in a jar with a tight cap. Shake to mix and keep chilled. Add 2 teaspoons of the prepared liquid to each cup of milk.

At ten or eleven months, baby will begin to show some interest in feeding himself. Encourage him by giving him a chicken bone to hold and crunch on, or a spoon of his very own to use at the beginning of a meal when he is eager to eat. You can finish up the feeding but he will slowly learn to handle a spoon and how to use it. Smile to show him your pleasure in his accomplishment. He will quickly learn also to eat carrot sticks or apple wedges or raw peas with his fingers.

If the family meals are well planned and nourishing, very soon the little one will be eating some of the good things from the family table.

Sometime after about one year, you may wish to introduce raw fertile egg yolk. Start with 1/16 of a teaspoon, and increase it just a tiny bit daily. You can add it to a bit of mashed avocado, or banana for variety. Baked potato may be served once a week now if you wish to add cooked foods. Mash with a little yogurt. Raw vegetables may be puréed in the blender, or very finely grated and added to mashed avocado, or thinned with a little carrot juice. Finely grated apple and carrot or apple and beet are good combinations.

Fresh, lightly steamed vegetables, puréed in the blender or pushed through a sieve and thinned with a little milk make very fine soups for little ones. Organically grown brown rice, baked sweet potato, or other complex starch foods may be served to the child over one year of age. Until that time the enzyme ptyalin, essential for the digestion of starch, is not present in the baby's saliva. A good hard crust of whole-grain bread is a help with teething. Raw kelp or lightly broiled fish, from a known source, may be chopped and soaked and the resulting liquid fed to the child for iodine and other sea minerals.

If you wish your child to have meat, and can find a safe source, it may be added to his diet after fourteen months (or before, if your doctor suggests it). It can be lightly broiled, then blended with a little water. When the child is older, he can eat a patty of broiled ground meat with his fingers. Organ meats, such as heart and sweetbreads, may be steamed, then finely chopped or ground. Fish, from a known safe source, is a good food for baby; steamed or broiled, and mashed or cut up to suit his age, it will add many essential minerals to his diet.

Homemade soups made from organically grown vegetables and safe chicken or meat, cooked at a very low temperature, may be puréed in your blender and frozen in ice-cube trays. Remove and store in a plastic bag tightly sealed in the freezer until needed.

Many vegetables may be finely grated and fed raw to the child eight months or older. (Before that time, grate raw vegetables and squeeze juice through a square of nylon net; feed only the juice to the baby.) Grated carrot, sweet potato, zucchini, parsnips, turnip, potato or rutabaga will be relished by almost every baby. Beets are good too, but very concentrated. Start with only a half teaspoon of grated beet, added to a food already established in the diet, such as banana or avocado.

Remember the little one's taste buds have not been perverted by sugar foods, spices and seasoning. Natural foods taste *good* all by themselves.

Be persistent about offering raw romaine and other salad greens so your child will grow up with a fondness for health-giving green salads. At first you can blend the greens in a bit of mineral water in the blender. Later they can be squashed through your grater before feeding and finally, when the baby's teeth are here, he can do his own chewing.

Any vegetable or fruit that you prepare for your family can be puréed or blended for the baby. Cook with very little water at the lowest possible temperature and use every drop of the cooking water. If the food is too thin, thicken with a little wheat germ. To prepare in advance, proceed as above then freeze in small cups or ice-cube trays. Store in a plastic bag in the freezer until needed. Remove from freezer and place in a small custard cup or other heat-proof dish to thaw. At meal time simply set the cup or dish in a pan of warm water until it is the proper temperature.

Fresh raw blender applesauce* or dried apricot sauce* may be served to the infant plain or blended into mashed banana.

Dried prunes should be soaked two days in the refrigerator—use apple juice to soak if you have it—then pit and purée in your blender (or put through a food grinder or mill if you have no blender). The prune sauce is luscious spooned over a scoop of yogurt or mixed with a tablespoonful or so of wheat germ. If sweetening is desired, use a bit of honey. *Sugar* is at the top of the "No No" list for both baby and mother.

Don't have any "junk" foods in the house, then they simply will not be available to the child, or to his parents.

WEANING

Every child sets his own timetable for weaning. Some babies nurse or drink from a bottle longer than others because they feel need for this security. Others, more adventurous and secure, look forward to drinking from a cup.

Withdrawing just one feeding from the daily schedule and offering milk from a cup at that meal only, is a gentle way to begin the weaning. A little extra attention and a loving cuddle or two during the day will make this time easier for the little one. The following week, if all goes well, another feeding can be withdrawn. As the child becomes more and more interested in the wonderful world around him and is enjoying at each meal a tummy full of hearty natural foods, he needs less nursing and usually tapers off to just a pre-bedtime snack. There is no harm in continuing this token feeding as long as the baby wants it. Even after the mother has considered the baby completely weaned, he may decide he wants to nurse a little "just for old times' sake." Usually he will be satisfied in a moment or two and this may well be his final nursing.

Most important to remember is that babies can actually *die* without a constant supply of love and loving— as well as milk.

Chapter IV

Feeding The Pre-Schooler

In feeding the pre-schooler we want to remember that food has more meaning in child growth and development than simply as a nutrient to permit growth and maintenance. Food serves an equally significant role in at least three areas of development.

Physically—In motor mastery of the body, eye, hand and mouth coordination, the complexities of swallowing and safe use of the mouth and throat muscles; in practice for future feeding and speech.

Mentally—Feeding is a potent learning process. The child puts everything in his mouth, not with the intention of eating everything he finds, but of learning about everything within mouth reach through the sound, taste, and feel perceived through the mouth.

Emotionally—Feeding is the primary interpersonal relationship with other people all through life. The infant learns about loving and being loved as he is nursed or held in his mother's arms to be fed.

Meal time for the pre-schooler should continue to be a pleasant time. Keep the servings small and, at least in the early months, offer just one food at a time in an unbreakable dish. Give him more of any food he enjoys and asks for, but don't coax or try to get him to eat more than he wants. No child ever starved himself to death!

Infant growth is so rapid and spectacular that many

times we are ill-prepared for the slower changes of the second and third year, and many times we try to press food on the child in an attempt to continue the large appetite and rapid rate of growth of the first year.

We need to understand the difference between "poor" and "small" appetite. Do not be so dismayed by the small quantity of food eaten that you offer all manner of nutritionally poor or even "junk" foods, just to get the child to eat something. Special care in the offering of high quality foods should be the rule.

Never allow your little ones to have carbonated drinks, candy or other harmful foods. What these "junk" foods do to the teeth is bad enough but what they do to the body and its vital functions is worse!

Be stern and firm with fond relatives or friends who come bearing gifts of candy, cookies or other "non" foods. Tell them your child's "tummy" is just barely big enough to hold all the *good* foods you want him to have.

A word here about illness. The pre-schooler often has many illnesses which are not a reflection on his care, but are due to his first encounters with communicable diseases.

Many times, the best food for a child is none at all. At the first sign of any illness, fever, sore throat, etc., *all* food should be withheld and only pure water should be given for a day or two. Fasting allows the body resources to work on the healing processes; energy used to digest and assimilate food hampers recovery. The child will have no appetite anyway but will require, instead of food: rest, sleep, peace and quiet, fresh air, and if the weather is nice, sunshine. These are nature's greatest healers, and they will often take care of simple illnesses without recourse to health-depleting shots and antibiotics.

Another thing we should remember is that some of the best childhood nutrition has probably been given in the form of small, frequent and wholesome feeding, while mother is preparing the family meals. Peas fresh from the pod, raw potatoes or carrots, bites of apples, raisins, or other raw fruits or vegetables will provide better quality nutrition than the finished cooked product at the dinner table. Food eaten with the fingers in happy companionship at mother's knee is good food.

Many pre-schoolers do well with a small, planned fourth meal at bedtime.

Do not be discouraged if your child does not learn at once to eat the good foods you would like him to eat. You came into the world with no food tastes developed. Remember you *learned* to like everything you enjoy now. Many mothers have a sad time trying to teach their youngsters to eat very bad foods.

Continue the codliver oil every day. The vegetables and fruits you prepare need not be grated or chopped as finely as for the younger child. You can now offer two kinds of food at once most of the time.

For a special breakfast treat, try a whole-grain or buckwheat yeast-raised pancake.* It can be topped with butter and raw applesauce* or a small amount of honey. Serve a small cup of milk or nut-milk if desired.

Lunch might include a green "finger" salad, home-made vegetable soup, a small serving of cottage cheese and milk. Other times serve banana pudding* and yogurt or fresh fruit diced and a cube of natural raw cheese.

Dinner is much the same as lunch. Carrot-pineapple (or other) grated salad, a lightly cooked or raw green leafy vegetable or a yellow vegetable, or a baked potato with yogurt. Fish, meat or cottage cheese—a small serving.

Desserts should be fruit most of the time with an occasional "jelled custard"* or a brown rice or millet pudding. Homemade ice cream* is a special treat. Yogurt topped with fresh fruit is a festive dessert too and most youngsters enjoy a carob pudding* once in a while.

Milk or yogurt may serve as a little bedtime snack, if one is desired.

Always use 100% whole grain in bread, cookies, pie

crust, hot or cold cereal and add extra wheat germ or soy flour.

Use only natural sweeteners such as raw honey, honey comb, molasses, sorghum, date sugar, real maple syrup, dried fruits and carob powder.

For the child four years and older, raw nuts may be soaked overnight in milk or pineapple juice and served with fruit or green salads.

Sunflower seeds and pumpkin seeds are just the right size for tiny fingers. My grandchildren like to mix raisins with them or cut up date-bits and raw sesame seeds. These are great to take along in individual waxed bags on hikes or on camping trips. Celery may be stuffed with peanut or other nut butters or sesame cheese spread.*

SUPER-SNACKS OR MEALTIME TREATS

Food offered as between-meal snacks should be high in quality and considered part of the daily nutrition. Most children will enjoy the following:

Honeycomb: instead of chewing gum. This is one of the richest known sources of the unsaturated fatty acids. It is to be chewed and enjoyed, then *swallowed;* the comb is perfectly digestible.

Popcorn: with raw butter or butter oil spread* and sea salt.

*Homemade ice cream** or *fruit sherbets:* fruit and yogurt popsicles* are delicious.

Celery: stuff with sesame cheese spread* or any nut butter.

Partly toasted nuts or seeds: Place ⅓ cup seeds or nuts on a cookie sheet and toast in a 250° oven until golden brown. Place at once in a jar with a tight lid. Add ⅔ cup raw seeds or nuts. Cover and shake a bit to mix well. Let stand for a few hours at room temperature and all the nuts or seeds will taste toasted.

Gelatin desserts: Fruit juices made into gelatin desserts, and molded in a tube cake pan, make a pretty birthday cake for the little one. Top with honey sweetened whipped cream and candles.

Birthday watermelon: Cut the melon in half lengthwise. Trim a thin slice from the rounded side, so the melon will sit on a platter or tray. Press the candles into the fruit in any pattern. Good for older children too; just get a bigger melon.

Sardines: Many dentists recommend the regular use of canned sardines in the child's diet. The small edible bones seem to provide calcium and other minerals to help developing teeth. A small mound of freshly prepared sweet potato or white potato topped with sweet butter, and two or three tiny sardines, make a fine lunch. Most children consider sardines finger foods. Most mothers do not.

Beverages: The best beverages for the growing child are the ones already part of his mealtimes. Milk—plain or with a teaspoon of molasses and a half teaspoon of brewer's yeast for a special treat. Raw fruit or vegetable juices, or juices canned without added sugar. Read the label carefully. Frozen juices are usually better suited to the child's needs. Here again, purchase pure fruit juices, not the ones labeled "juice drinks." Home-canned fruit and vegetable juices are fine for baby too, especially if you grow your own poison-free foods or can purchase them in your area.

Salad sandwiches: Place a slice of raw cheddar or jack cheese between slices of zucchini or turnip. Spread apple or pear wedges with peanut butter or sesame cheese spread. Roll lettuce leaf up with cottage cheese filling. Finger lengths of celery may be stuffed with mixed peanut butter and cottage cheese. Slices of raw vegetables such as cucumber, turnip or zucchini may be cut in special shapes—stars, bells or Christmas trees, numbers, or letters (of the child's name etc.). Top with a dab of mashed avocado or nut butter.

Calf's heart: Buy calf's heart; wash, slice crosswise into rounds. Broil lightly on each side, or have your butcher grind beef heart into hamburger meat (⅓ heart, ⅔ beef): add egg and seasoning and shape into patties for broiling.

Frozen bananas: Bananas, cut in half crosswise and frozen on a stick, are very good. Place on a cookie sheet lined with waxed paper to freeze. Dip in melted carob bar for an extra special treat. You can buy the wooden sticks in the paper goods section of your department store.

Avocados: Although classed as a fruit, the avocado provides more energy and nutrients, pound for pound, than almost any other food. Its digestibility approaches that of whole raw milk. Many minerals and the vitamins A, B, C, D, E and K are all contained in this blessed fruit. A good quantity of a high quality protein and a naturally unsaturated fat lie safe and protected within its unsprayed green covering. They are bland enough to blend with other flavors but have a delightful flavor of their own.

Mash and pile on a baked potato or use as a dip with carrot and celery sticks. Spread on small fingers of whole grain bread or toast. Dice and serve with a toothpick for a handy "spear," or dilute with milk for an instant avocado cream soup.* Add a drizzle of honey and a bit of fruit juice or purée to the mashed avocado and there is dessert! Surely this fine natural food should be served often in the menu of both the child and adult.

> NOTE: Purchase the fruit hard and green at your market and place in a dark, warm place to ripen. It is spoon-ready when the fruit yields to gentle pressure between the palms of the hands.

Beets: Baby beets lightly steamed and served on a toothpick are easy to eat. Raw baby beets can be served as finger foods. Just don't watch!

Pushers: Tiny raw asparagus spears, or sturdy stalks of chard or kale, make fine edible "pushers" to help get other food onto the fork or spoon.

Pineapple tidbits: Cut fresh pineapple into one-inch squares. Dip in honey, then in crushed nuts or shredded coconut. Freeze until ready to serve. Bananas may be sliced in one-inch sections and served as above.

HELPFUL SUGGESTIONS

Fruits—Vegetables: Obtain organically grown fruits and vegetables as often as possible, or grow your own. When necessary to use commercially grown varieties, add a good vitamin-mineral supplement to the child's diet.

Supplementary amounts of vitamins E or A: To help a child take supplementary amounts of vitamins A or E, open a capsule with a needle, pour into a spoon of honeycomb or honey; mix well and serve. You may use this method for wheat germ oil also.

Cod liver oil: Cod liver oil is easy to take from a spoon. Have oil and spoon ice cold, in refrigerator. Follow with a swallow of milk or juice.

Pure water: Be sure your supply of water is safe and free of nitrates. Baby's tiny liver cannot detoxify chemicals or poisons as well as a grown-up liver can. If in doubt, have water tested by the Health Department.

Between-meal snacking: No eating between meals, except for small meals planned as part of the daily nutrition, or on Super-Special occasions. The mouth needs to remain empty for periods of three to four hours at a time, so the natural acids in the saliva can cleanse and protect the teeth.

How much is enough? Give your little chow hound as much or as little whole grain cereal, as much or as little fruit or vegetable or as much or as little yogurt, cottage cheese, egg or meat as he enjoys eating. Some days he will eat anything and everything; then there will be meals—even whole days—when he will mysteriously refuse to eat any or all of his foods. He may say to you, as my youngest granddaughter said to me recently, "I *can't* like applesauce this morning, Nana." Learn to respect his judgment and to remove the food promptly. Sometimes he may be cutting teeth or just not feeling up to par. When he has finished what he will eat willingly, take him out of the high-chair, without comment, not to *see* food again until the next mealtime.

WARNING: Keep all detergents, bleach, paints, poison sprays, cleaners, turpentine, aspirin and other medicines safely out of reach of your toddler. To a baby, *everything* that can be opened is to *eat* or *drink* and enough of a harmful substance can go down that tender gullet in one exploratory gulp to do drastic harm. Each year hundreds of children die from drinking or eating such substances. Do *not* leave your baby near such items even for a moment while you answer the telephone, go to the door, or turn the fire out under a kettle on the stove. Take the baby with you or place the object well out of reach. Do not give your baby aspirin or "baby aspirin," except under the supervision of your doctor. Many young children and babies die each year from an accidental overdose of this drug.

Car, air or sea sickness: If your child is troubled with "car sickness" or "air sickness," many mothers have found that this can be prevented if the child's diet is adequately supplied with vitamin B^6. To use, crush and dissolve a 25 milligram tablet of B^6 in water. Add to juice or other beverage before starting to travel. Foods containing B^6 are: heart, kidney, brewer's yeast, honey, egg yolk, cabbage and pecans. If more of these foods are included in your child's diet daily, this troublesome illness may never occur. Of course if *extra* B^6 is given, you must make doubly sure that all the other parts of the B complex are well supplied, otherwise a deficiency may be created. A little brewer's yeast may be stirred into the juice *with* the extra B^6, then all the other parts of the B vitamin "family" will be taken at the same time.

The mind needs feeding too! Everything said to a child, from the moment of birth, is registered in the little one's brain. Words of love, encouragement, praise and appreciation bring delight and joy to your child, long before he actually *knows* the meaning of such words. So let your praise be lavish, your words of love unlimited. Appreciate, out loud, each new accomplishment, each lesson learned. If your baby *knows* that you think he is a pretty fine fellow, he will quite likely grow up thinking you are right.

IN CONCLUSION

The most important part of eating to a child is the warm social interchange. To him the nutritional aspect of food is secondary. With a cheerful, unhurried mother and a contented child, mealtime can be what it should be—the happiest time of the day. Relax and enjoy your precious child. Love him a lot and do the best you can, knowing that food served with affection and care will do wonders while you are learning to do better.

PART TWO

RECIPES

Chapter V

Foods for Infants and Children

BEVERAGES

MINERAL-RICH WATER FOR BABY

½ cup organically grown almonds with the skins
¼ cup oat groats or flakes
¼ cup organically grown raisins

Place in a quart jar and cover with pure water. Soak for two days in the refrigerator. Strain the liquid and keep cold in a covered jar. This may be warmed to room temperature and offered to baby to drink from the tip of a spoon or in a bottle whenever necessary. Very rich in iron and other vital minerals. The soaked almonds and raisins may be added to the family cereal or salads.

When your baby is five or six months old, his own store of iron becomes depleted. You may add even more available *iron* to this recipe by adding 1 tablespoon unsulphured molasses to the strained liquid.

NOTE: Organically grown almond skins contain a natural enzyme to protect them from insects. This enzyme will also protect the infant from worms, or if the child does become infected, increase the use of this mineral-rich water to 6 tablespoons daily—more for an older child. The enzyme will safely digest the worms and their eggs, thus making the use of dangerous drug unnecessary.

NUT AND SEED MILK

  1 cup almonds (organically grown if possible)
  ¼ cup sesame or sunflower seeds
  2 cups water

Soak in a cool place for several hours or overnight, then place in blender. Run on high for three minutes. Add: 1 tablespoon raw honey or unsulphured molasses. Blend briefly. Strain through a very fine strainer or through three layers of nylon net. Reserve the nut-seed residue for salads or other dishes. Add to the strained milk 2 cups more water. Keep chilled until ready to serve.

To use for an infant *formula*, make *exactly* the same each time, measuring accurately. *More* water may be needed when the baby is very young and *less* as he grows older and needs a more concentrated food. Your pediatrician can guide you in this. You may also add as the child grows, any or all of these supplemental foods: ½ teaspoon dulse or kelp powder, 1 tablespoon soy milk powder, or 1 teaspoon or more brewer's yeast. Add *one* at a time, and wait at least five days to see how the child handles each new food before adding any other.

MOLASSES BEVERAGE For Toddlers

  1 teaspoon molasses
  1 cup milk—warmed slightly or cold

Mix and serve.

GREEN DRINK

Place in blender—1 cup pineapple juice, raw, frozen or canned (unsweetened)—add a mixture of 2 or more greens that have been washed and their woody stems removed. Push down lightly until blender is about half-full.

Blend until finely ground, then add 2 or 3 cups more juice. Let stand on ground leaves for 5 minutes. This gives the enzyme in the juice time to release more of the green chlorophyll. This makes about 4 cups.

Strain and serve or chill and serve in your prettiest crystal goblets as a party drink. For greens, always use a little mint if you have it for its delicious taste, plus any sprouted seed greens such as alfalfa or mung bean sprouts. Then add any greens in season such as collards, chard, kale, lettuce, spinach, comfrey or parsley. Alfalfa is good too, so are the *wild* greens such as malva, dandelion, fillaree, mustard, chickweed or other edible weeds. *Small* quantities may be used of watercress, radish or carrot tops or other strong-tasting greens.

A handful of sunflower or pumpkin seeds may be added and a date or two for a drink that is practically a meal-in-a-glass. This you would not strain.

SUPER-SHAKE

1½ cups pineapple juice
2 carrots, cut up finely
1 apple—cored and cut up
1 tablespoon of honey

Blend well, then begin adding ice cubes, until thick. For some blenders, it will be necessary to wrap the ice cubes in a tea towel and crush with a mallet. Serves 4.

TOMATO-GREEN DRINK

2 cups fresh or canned tomato juice
2 cups greens—parsley and kale or beet leaves are good
2 leaves fresh sweet basil, or
½ teaspoon dried sweet basil leaves

Blend, chill and serve. Serves 4.

MELON SEED DRINK

Save pulp and seeds from the center of cantaloupes, or other melons until you have 2 cups of the seed and pulp mixture. Place seeds in blender with 1 cup pineapple or apple juice. Blend until creamy. Strain and chill. Now add to blender 1 cup more juice and 1 cup green leaves, part of which can be mint for flavor. Chard, spinach, alfalfa sprouts or any greens in season can be used. Add ½ lemon and peel. Blend until well mixed.

Add 1 teaspoon or more honey to flavor if desired. Combine with seed milk. For the older child or adults, just mix and serve. Serves 4-6.

BOYSENBERRY-KEFIR DRINK

1 pint frozen boysenberries, without sugar
1 quart kefir, a cultured milk drink
(If kefir is unavailable, use 1 quart of yogurt
  stirred until it is smooth.)

Blend berries until smooth in blender and strain if you desire. There are valuable nutrients in the seeds. Sweeten with 1 tablespoon honey and slowly add to kefir or yogurt. Makes a fine between-meal snack. Serves 6.

RHUBARB JUICE DRINK

Juice fresh rhubarb and blend with twice as much fresh apple juice for a beverage both beautiful and delicious. Add a little honey to sweeten, if desired.

Or, make in blender. Place in blender bowl:

2 cups apple juice
6 stalks fresh rhubarb, cut in 1-inch lengths.

Blend, add 1 tablespoon honey and blend again.
Strain and serve. Serves 6.

HOMEMADE VEGETABLE COCKTAIL

2 cups fresh tomatoes (or home canned
  tomatoes or juice)
½ beet—cut in pieces
½ cup carrot pieces
½ cup celery pieces or leaves
Wedge of lettuce
Piece of cabbage
Piece of onion or onion tops
Handful of parsley
Pieces of red or green peppers

Blend well, then add cracked ice cubes to chill as you serve it. Use any vegetable from your garden and your favorite herbs to flavor. Serves 6.

CRANBERRY-APPLE NECTAR

Place in blender:

- 2 cups apple juice or unsweetened canned pineapple juice
- 1½ cups raw cranberries
- ¼ orange (use rind if organically grown)
- 2 tablespoons honey

Blend for three minutes—let set 10 minutes—strain. Reserve cranberries for relish or gelatin dessert. Add to juice, 2 cups more juice. Chill and serve. A colorful fruit drink for the holidays or a pretty breakfast drink anytime. Serves 6-8.

SUMMER COOLER

Place in blender:

- 2 cups pineapple juice
- 1 cup fresh asparagus spears or
- ½ cup each asparagus and cucumber

Blend two minutes—add 1 tablespoon lemon juice or to taste. Serves 4.

HONEY EGGNOG

- 3 eggs, fertile, if possible
- 1 tablespoon honey or 2 tablespoons molasses
- ¼ teaspoon sea salt or kelp
- 2 cups certified raw milk, or milk and cream, or skim milk or nut-milk
- 1 teaspoon vanilla or orange extract

Beat eggs until very light and thick (with beater or in a blender). Add honey or molasses, salt, vanilla and milk and beat again. Serve with a dusting of nutmeg over the top. Makes three or four servings.

BANANA EGGNOG

Add one mashed banana to the above, in the blender or beat well. Serves four.

AVOCADO EGGNOG

3 eggs
1 tablespoon honey
1/4 teaspoon sea salt or kelp
2 cups milk
1 tablespoon grated orange rind
1/4 cup avocado—peeled, seeded and mashed

Beat egg yolks with milk and avocado. Add honey, orange rind and kelp. Blend well. Beat the egg whites until stiff and fold into milk mixture. Dust with nutmeg. Makes three or four servings.

NOTE: If safe fertile eggs are not available, you may use eggs from other sources if they are firm shelled—not cracked. To guard against salmonella, wash them in a diluted solution of liquid household bleach (1 teaspoon bleach to a pint of water) before using. Wash all such eggs as soon as purchased and store in the refrigerator.

INSTANT LUNCH

1/2 cup apple juice
1 egg
2 dates
1/2 apple
Optional: 1 teaspoon acidophilus concentrate or
1 teaspoon brewer's yeast

Serves 2.

CARROT MILK BEVERAGE

1 cup nut or seed or soy milk or other milk
2 carrots, cut in small pieces

Place in blender and liquefy. Serve chilled or heat gently and serve in mugs. Great for the little ones. Serves 2.

BLENDER FOODS FOR BABIES

BANANA SMOOTHIE

1 fresh ripe banana (deep yellow with
   brown flecked skin)
½ pear
¼ avocado
Enough apple or pineapple juice to engage the blender
blades.

For the older child, sprinkle with raw wheat germ in
the serving dish.

GOLDEN APPLE LUNCHEON

½ apple
½ carrot
½ banana
1 tablespoon sunflower seeds
Enough juice to blend

PAPAYA-RAISIN SUPPER

¼ papaya, small
¼ avocado, small
¼ cup raisins or pitted prunes
½ cup yogurt
Blend

VEGETABLE-AVOCADO DRINK

½ avocado
¼ cup yogurt
¼ cup raw peas
¼ carrot. Blend, then stir in
1 tablespoon wheat germ

APRICOT-AVOCADO SOUP

Soak 6 dried apricots in ¼ cup water or apple juice
Place in blender with
   ¼ avocado—peeled, seeded and diced
   1 tablespoon almond butter
   ½ apple, washed and cored

Blend until well mixed. For the toddler, add wheat
germ to thicken.

CARROT LOAF

½ cup finely grated carrots
½ cup finely shredded zucchini
1 tablespoon yogurt
1 tablespoon peanut butter or other nut butter

Blend yogurt and peanut butter. Mix in vegetables. Press into your ¼ cup measure or an ice cream scoop. Turn out on serving dishes. Makes 2 or 3 servings.

PARSNIP LUNCHEON

1 cup parsnips, washed and cut in small pieces
¼ cup carrot, washed and sliced
½ avocado or ¼ cup yogurt
2 tablespoons almond butter
¼ teaspoon kelp powder
¼ teaspoon brewer's yeast

Place vegetables in blender and run until smooth. Add almond butter and seasonings and run again. Makes 4 servings.

PAPAYA TOPPING

1 small papaya, peeled and seeded
2 teaspoons lemon juice
4 teaspoons honey

Place all in blender and run until smooth. Good over plain yogurt or custard. If any is left over, pour into a custard cup—cover and chill. The next day you will have a lovely mold of "papaya jelly." Makes 4 servings.

Note: Save the seeds, blend, and add to grown-ups' salad dressing.

GREEN LIMAS for BABY

In blender place:
½ avocado
1 cup fresh green lima beans, or
½ package frozen lima beans
1 tablespoon broth or juice
¼ teaspoon kelp powder

Blend until smooth. If too thick, add yogurt; if you wish a thicker mixture, add a little wheat germ. Makes 4 servings.

GREEN PEAS WITH ALMOND BUTTER

1 cup fresh peas, or
½ package frozen peas
2 sprigs of parsley
2 tablespoons almond butter
½ carrot
2 tablespoons tomato juice, or more as needed

Place peas and parsley in blender. Add enough tomato juice to cover the blades. Blend until smooth. Add almond butter and blend briefly again. Thicken with wheat germ, if desired. For variety, ½ medium carrot may be added at times. Makes 4 servings.

CORN CHOWDER

1 cup fresh corn, or
½ package frozen corn
2 tablespoons tomato juice, or broth, or enough to make a soup as thin as desired.
½ avocado, peeled, seeded and diced
¼ teaspoon kelp

Blend corn with tomato juice until liquefied and creamy. Add avocado and kelp. This may be warmed just to serving temperature.

AVOCADO-SPINACH SOUP

Place in blender:
1 peeled and cut up ripe avocado
¾ cup fresh spinach
¼ cup parsley (use only the tender leaves)
1 cup chicken or beef broth
Blend until smooth, then add:
¾ cup certified raw milk or cream and milk or nut milk sea salt and pepper to taste
½ teaspoon Yerba Encanta, Vege-Sal, or any other herbed seasoning found in health food stores.

Chill and serve cold. For a hot soup, warm just to serving temperature and serve in a warm bowl. Makes four servings.

AVOCADO CREAM SOUP

2 cups certified raw milk or other milk—nut
    milk is good!
1 large ripe avocado

Mash peeled and seeded avocado in bowl or with blender. Slowly add milk. Season to taste with Yerba Encanta or other herbed seasoning. Add ½ teaspoon sea salt or dulse. Heat just to serving temperature. Very good for your toddler or pre-schooler. Serves 4.

BLENDER SOUP for BABY

½ cup homemade bone broth—warm
½ carrot
1 stalk asparagus or celery
¼ sweet potato

Blend well. Thicken with 1 tablespoon wheat germ to serve.

YOGURT-PRUNE PUDDING

½ cup prune juice, or more, to make sauce as
    thin as you wish
3 large pitted prunes, soaked
6 large pitted dates

Place all in blender and run until smooth. Serve over plain yogurt. Makes 1 cup.

CAROB-PRUNE DESSERT

½ cup prune juice
2 teaspoons honey
1 teaspoon carob powder
1 tablespoon grated coconut
Sprinkle of cinnamon

Place in blender and run until creamy. Serve over yogurt, custard or, for special occasions, over ice cream. Makes ¾ cup.

BERRY DESSERT for BABY

1 cup red raspberries or strawberries (fresh or frozen
    without sugar)
¼ cup apple juice
1 teaspoon honey, or more

Blend together until smooth. Strain out seeds for
younger children. For three-year-olds and over, a portion of the seeds may be returned to the sauce.

Serve over plain yogurt or jelled or baked custard.
Makes 4 servings.

DRIED APRICOT SAUCE

2 cups apple or pineapple juice
1 cup dried apricots, unsulphured
2 tablespoons grated orange rind
1 tablespoon honey
¼ teaspoon cloves (omit for younger children)
Several apricot kernels (optional)

Soak apricots in juice overnight. Next day place with
juice in blender and run 3 minutes. Season with cloves,
orange rind and honey. Makes 2½ cups.

FIRST SALADS FOR TODDLERS

1. Grate carrot on a very fine grater (i.e., nutmeg),
add ½ teaspoon lemon juice mixed with 1 tablespoon
cream.

2. Cut up ½ fully ripe, fresh tomato. Crush with a
fork, add ½ teaspoon lemon juice and 1 tablespoon cream
or ½ teaspoon salad oil.

3. Mix oil or cream in a bowl and grate into it,
equal parts fresh carrot and fresh apple. Stir and serve
at once. ¾ apple and ¼ *finely* grated beet is a good mixture.

4. Finely chopped alfalfa sprouts with grated carrot,
mix with pineapple juice.

5. Mung bean sprouts, finely diced red sweet pepper, moisten with fresh orange juice.

6. Finely grated raw potato and apple. Dress with yogurt and ½ teaspoon honey.

7. Finely grated apple. Mix with well mashed banana.

8. Mash ½ ripe pear. Add grated apple and yogurt to mix.

9. Fresh peach—mashed with grated apple and a little orange juice.

10. Mashed papaya with grated apple and yogurt:

11. Mashed avocado with grated apple and orange juice for dressing.

12. Mashed avocado with grated carrot, and lemon juice.

MISCELLANEOUS FOODS

JELLED CUSTARD

```
3  cups milk—certified raw, if possible
⅓  cup honey
4  eggs, plus
2  egg yolks
¼  teaspoon sea salt or kelp
1  teaspoon vanilla
3  tablespoons grated orange or lemon rind
2  tablespoons gelatin
Nutmeg
```

Dissolve gelatin in ¼ cup milk in small saucepan. Melt over low heat, stirring constantly. Beat eggs and egg yolks with rotary beater or in blender till well mixed. Add sea salt, vanilla, orange rind and dissolved gelatin and remainder of milk.

Pour into six 6 oz. custard cups, dust with nutmeg and set in the refrigerator until jelled. Serve with whipped cream topping* or pouring cream. For a richer custard use 1 cup cream in place of 1 cup of the milk. May be unmolded onto serving dish if desired. Serves 6.

BAKED HONEY CUSTARDS

Use same ingredients as above except for gelatin.

1. Heat milk very slowly in a medium-size saucepan, rinsed first with cold water.

2. Beat eggs and egg yolks slightly in a large bowl; stir in honey, salt, vanilla and orange rind; slowly add scalded milk. Strain into a 4-cup measure or pitcher; pour into 6 buttered 6 oz. custard cups, or a quart size casserole or baking dish. Set cups or pan in a large pan; pour boiling water in the pan to a depth of 1 inch.

3. Sprinkle with nutmeg. Place pan in slow oven 325°F. Bake until center is almost set. About 30 to 40 minutes for the small cups. Serve warm or chilled. Serves 6.

CHICKEN CUSTARD

1½ cup diced cooked chicken
1 cup whole wheat bread crumbs
½ cup grated cheese
2 eggs, beaten
3 tablespoons cream or milk
1 tablespoon chopped parsley
¼ teaspoon sea salt
¼ teaspoon poultry seasoning

Mix lightly. Place in 4 well-buttered custard cups. Set in baking pan with 1 inch of hot water in the bottom. Bake at 350°F. for 30 minutes. This may also be baked in a glass baking dish or loaf pan. Makes 4 servings.

SWEET POTATO CUSTARD

1 cup sweet potato purée
2 eggs, slightly beaten
2 tablespoons milk or cream
1 teaspoon butter, melted

Combine all ingredients. Pour into 4 buttered custard cups and place in a kettle with gently boiling water. Cover and steam 20 minutes. Mashed squash, rutabaga, or carrots may be used in this dish. Makes 4 servings.

SWEETBREADS

Freeze a pair of veal or beef sweetbreads. Slice thin, dip in brown-rice flour or whole-wheat flour with a little sea salt. Quickly sauté on each side in a fry pan with a little melted butter.

Remove the membrane from around the outside of each slice. Cut into small cubes and give your toddler a toothpick for a "spear." Serves 4.

VEGETABLE PURÉE for BABY

Use any lightly cooked vegetable. Place in blender bowl:

    ¼ cup vegetable juice or soup broth
    ½ cup of the vegetable

Cover and turn on machine until thoroughly blended. Remove cover, add ½ cup more vegetable. Run again. If thick purée is desired (for older children) use ¾ to 1 cup vegetable for the addition.

SWEET POTATO WITH AVOCADO

    2 baked sweet potatoes, cut in half. Reserve shells,
        scoop out centers and mash with
    1 tablespoon butter. Add
    ½ cup mashed avocado

For the older children and grown-ups, fill reserved shells and heat in a moderate oven for 5 minutes.

Steamed squash or pumpkin may be served in the above recipe in place of the sweet potato. Serves 4.

BABY SCALLOPS

Simmer gently in covered kettle:

    6 scallops
    1 tablespoon broth or water

When tender, dice and season with a bit of butter and a sprinkle of kelp.

Serve with a toothpick to spear. Makes 2 servings.

STEAMED GREENS

3 cups spinach, washed and chopped. Place 2 cups prepared spinach in kettle with tight lid. Bring to boil. At *once* lower the heat below boiling and simmer 2 minutes. Meanwhile chop remaining 1 cup spinach very *fine*—add to cooked spinach, stir to mix well. Season with fresh butter or cream and serve. Makes 4 servings.

Other greens may be prepared in this fashion—chard, collards, kale, chicory, beet leaf and endive, etc. Finely chopped parsley may be used as *part* of the cup of raw greens for flavor or 2 or 3 tablespoons onion, diced, may be cooked sometimes with the greens.

SCALLOPED TURNIPS

2 turnips, shredded—use skin if tender
Warm milk to cover
½ cup whole wheat bread crumbs
2 tablespoons grated cheddar cheese

Place turnips in small buttered casserole. Add warm milk. Sprinkle with bread crumbs. Cover and bake until turnips are just barely tender. Remove cover and top with grated cheese. Leave in oven 1 minute to melt cheese, then serve. Serves 4.

Carrots, rutabagas or parsnips may be used in place of turnips.

RAW VEGETABLE SOUP

Place in blender:
1 tomato
1 teaspoon honeycomb
½ cucumber
Juice of ½ lemon
¼ small beet, sliced
2 tablespoons yogurt
1 small green onion
½ carrot, diced
¼ potato
2 cabbage leaves
3 spinach or chard leaves
1 teaspoon soy sauce
½ cup chicken or beef broth, or
     vegetable cooking water

Liquefy till smooth and creamy. Warm to serving temperature—below 120°F. Any vegetables in season may be used. Makes 4 servings.

POTATO PORRIDGE

1 cup water—boiling
1 teaspoon sea salt or dulse
1 potato, scrubbed but not peeled

Quickly grate the potato into the boiling water, add the sea salt or dulse; remove from the stove. Cover and let stand about five minutes.

Serve with butter and, if desired, a little honey.

A fine supper dish for little folks, or even big folks. Makes 2 or 3 servings.

BEGINNER'S MUESLI CEREAL
(For 1 year old and older)

1 tablespoon oat flakes
1 teaspoon wheat germ
2 tablespoons apple juice or water

Soak overnight—next morning add:
1 teaspoon lemon juice
½ large apple, grated (use skin for older child)
1 tablespoon cream or nut milk, mixed with
1 teaspoon almond butter

TEETHING COOKIES FOR BABY

2 tablespoons honey
1 tablespoon molasses
2 tablespoons oil
1 egg yolk, beaten
½ cup soy flour
¼ cup wheat germ
½ cup whole wheat flour

Stir together the honey, molasses, oil and egg yolk. Add the mixed flours and enough wheat germ to make a stiff dough. Since flours differ, if too thick, add a tablespoon of milk. If too soft, add a bit more soy flour. Roll dough into ¼ inch thickness. Cut into rectangles 1x1½ inches. Place on ungreased cookie sheet. Bake at 350°F. until golden brown, about 15 to 20 minutes.

Makes four dozen cookies.

NOTE: Do not use until your baby has been *started* on *every* food used in the recipe.

SPECIAL OCCASION TREATS

DATE-NUT BALLS

1 cup dates, pitted
¼ cup raisins
1 cup pecans

Put all ingredients through food grinder. Form into small balls. Roll in grated coconut or dried milk powder (non-instant). Makes 2 dozen balls.

APRICOT CONFECTION

1 cup dried apricots
½ cup sunflower seeds
6 dates, pitted

Grind fruits and seeds. Form into small logs; roll in chopped nuts. You may instead form one larger roll. Chill and cut in slices with a wet knife. Makes 12 small logs or 12 slices.

CAROB NUT SQUARES

1 cup pecans
¼ cup carob powder
¼ cup sunflower seeds
¼ cup wheat germ
1 cup dates, pitted

Grind dates, nuts and sunflower seeds together. Add wheat germ and coconut. Press into a baking dish lined with chopped nuts. Cut in squares. Makes 12-15 servings.

HIGH PROTEIN ICE CREAM

    4 eggs
    1 cup milk
    1 banana (or 1 cup berries)

Place in blender and turn 2 minutes, or beat eggs well with rotary beater then add milk and fruit. Now add

    1 teaspoon vanilla
    2 tablespoons honey
    ⅓ cup protein supplement
    ¼ cup safflower oil. Beat again, then add
    2 cups heavy cream

Mix well. Freeze in a 2-quart freezer or pour into 2 deep freezing trays and freeze in the deep freeze. Stir once during freezing or beat well for fluffy, smooth ice cream. Freeze until firm. Makes 10-12 servings.

BANANA PUDDING

    1 large golden ripe banana
    1 egg yolk, from fertile egg
    1 drop vanilla, if desired

Mash banana, add yolk, and blend until smooth. Dip into serving dishes. Top with cream, or whipped cream, coconut or nuts (chopped) or yogurt. Some youngsters like it best plain or with just a sprinkle of nutmeg. Makes a fine breakfast or supper. This may also be made with papaya. Makes 1 or 2 servings.

OATMEAL COOKIES

    ½ cup honey or molasses
    ½ cup salad oil
    3 eggs, beaten
    ½ teaspoon cinnamon
    ½ teaspoon allspice
    1 teaspoon baking powder (buy at health food store)
    1 cup oatmeal
    ¼ cup wheat germ
    ¼ cup soy flour
    1 cup whole wheat flour
    1 cup chopped raisins or dates
    1 cup chopped nuts

Mix honey and oil; stir in beaten eggs. Mix dry ingredients together and stir in gradually; last, add nuts and dates. Drop by tablespoons on a lightly oiled baking sheet. Bake at 375°F. until golden brown. Makes 4 dozen cookies.

CAROB COOKIES

    2 cups dates, pitted
    1 cup raisins
    1 cup nuts, pecans or other
    ¼ cup carob powder
    ¼ cup sesame seeds

Grind dates, raisins and nuts. Mix well; add carob powder and sesame seeds. Shape into little cookies and chill. Makes 4 dozen cookies.

BRAZIL NUT COOKIES

    1 cup Brazil nuts
    1 cup pecans or walnuts
    1 cup dates
    1 cup raisins
    1 teaspoon vanilla
    1 tablespoon honey

Put nuts and fruit through food grinder twice. Add vanilla and honey the second time. Form into a long roll. Chill and slice with a wet knife. Makes 36 servings.

PICNIC PUNCH

    2 quarts fresh apple juice, chilled
    1 cup unsweetened pineapple juice
    1 box fresh-frozen red raspberries
    6 crushed mint leaves

Mix in gallon container and wrap with many layers of newspaper to keep chilled until you reach the picnic site.

JUICE POPSICLES

    2 cups fresh apple or grape juice
    1 cup left-over juice from home-canned cherries,
        apricots, pears or peaches

Pour into popsicle molds or deep ice-cube trays and freeze. Wooden handles or spoons may be placed in the popsicle when almost frozen. For a different flavor, add 1 cup yogurt to the above recipe and a little honey to sweeten if needed. Makes six ½ cup size popsicles.

SQUASH OR PUMPKIN SEED SNACK

Save seeds from banana squash, butternut squash, "spaghetti squash" or other varieties. Place seeds in a thin layer on lightly oiled cooking sheet. Leave some of the strings and pulp on the seeds for sweetness and flavor. Toast in a low 250°F. oven until golden brown. Season as desired with sea salt and herbed seasoning. Older children and parents may enjoy a little garlic on them or a bit of paprika.

Chapter VI

Foods for the Family

BEVERAGES

MOLASSES BEVERAGE For Grown-ups

1 tablespoon unsulphured molasses
½ teaspoon cereal or chicory coffee replacement
  (optional) such as Sano-Caff, Pero-Figo, etc.

Pour boiling water in cup. Add molasses and cereal "coffee" if desired. Serve with milk or cream.

RASPBERRY LEAF-MINT TEA

1 tablespoon raspberry leaves
1 cup mint leaves
2 sprigs lemon grass or parsley

Remove stems from mint leaves. Place all in a teapot and cover with boiling water. Let steep in a warm place 10 minutes. Sweeten with honey, if desired.

BUTTERMILK-TOMATO COOLER

1 cup tomato juice, fresh or canned
1 cup buttermilk or
1 cup yogurt, stirred until smooth

Stir tomato juice into the buttermilk: chill and serve.

BREADS AND CEREALS

CRUNCHY BREAKFAST CEREAL OR SNACK

¼ cup sesame seeds
4 cups rolled oats
1 cup rolled rye or wheat
1 cup wheat germ
½ cup corn meal or soy grits
½ cup coconut flakes
1 cup chopped nuts (almonds, pecans, filberts)
½ teaspoon sea salt
1 teaspoon vanilla

Method No. 1. Add to the above ingredients ½ cup yellow D brown sugar. Combine, in a rimmed baking pan about 10 x 15 inches, all ingredients but vanilla. Mix well. Sprinkle vanilla over all and stir again. Spread in an even layer. Bake at 250°F. for about 50 minutes or until the coconut is a light toasty brown. Stir about every 10 minutes. Cool.

Method No. 2. Melt in small kettle ¼ pound butter. Add vanilla and ½ cup honey, sorghum or brown sugar. Place dry ingredients in a large rimmed baking pan. Add honey, butter mixture and mix thoroughly. Bake at 250°F. for about 50 minutes or until coconut is light brown. Stir about every 10 minutes with a long handled spoon. Cool. Add to either variety after cooling, ½ cup sunflower seeds, 1 cup raisins or cut up dates.

Store in a tightly closed container in a cool place. Great to take camping! Makes about 40–¼ cup servings,

SUPER-CEREAL

Grind in a little nut mill or a blender, one at a time:
4 tablespoons each of sunflower seeds, pumpkin seeds, flax seeds, almonds and cashews or filberts. Add:
2 tablespoons ground sesame seeds
4 tablespoons wheat germ
4 tablespoons lecithin granules

If you do not have some of the ingredients, just add more of the others. Place in a covered jar in the refrigerator. Serves 4.

To serve:

The night before, put 4 tablespoons old-fashioned rolled oat flakes to soak in 8 tablespoons pineapple or apple juice. In the morning, place 2 tablespoons soaked oats in the bottom of each serving dish, and for each serving add:

> 1 medium sized apple or pear, finely grated or sliced, or other fruit in season
> 1 teaspoon date sugar or honey
> 4 tablespoons cereal mix
> Add cream or yogurt as desired.

FLAXSEED CEREAL

Heat 2 cups of water to boiling, and stir in slowly,
> 1 to 1¼ cups coarsely ground flaxseed, or flaxseed meal. Add
> 1 teaspoon dulse or ½ teaspoon sea salt

Remove from heat at once. Cover and let stand five minutes. Now add:

> 1 cup chopped dates or raisins
> ½ cup chopped nuts

Cover again for a few minutes. Serve with milk or cream or nut milk. Add honey if desired. Very helpful for normal bowel action during pregnancy. Makes 4-6 servings.

CORNBREAD—YEAST-RAISED

> 2 tablespoons dried yeast, or 2 cakes
> ½ cup lukewarm water or potato cooking water
> ½ cup honey or molasses
> 2 cups milk
> 2 teaspoons sea salt or dulse
> 4 eggs, beaten
> 1½ cups whole wheat flour
> 1½ cups whole cornmeal
> ½ cup wheat germ
> ½ cup soy flour
> ½ cup salad oil

Soak yeast in warm water for 5 minutes. Add honey. Pour into a large mixing bowl and add milk, salt and eggs. Stir all dry ingredients together and gradually add to milk mixture. Mix well. Add oil and stir again.

Pour into two 9x9x2" pans, buttered. Let rise in a warm place until up to the top of the pan (about 30 minutes). Preheat oven to 400°F. As you put the bread in the oven, turn the heat back to 375°F. Bake until golden brown. Serve hot with butter. One pan may be covered with plastic wrap and placed in the freezer until needed. Each pan makes 12 servings.

WHOLE GRAIN CRACKERS

    1 cup rolled oats or wheat
    ½ cup whole wheat flour
    ½ cup wheat germ
    ½ cup soy flour
    ½ cup water mixed with ¾ cup oil
    ½ teaspoon salt
    Sesame seeds—optional

Mix dry ingredients; add oil and water. Stir well. Roll dough out very thick. Sprinkle with sesame seeds, if desired. Cut in squares. Bake at 350°F. for 30 minutes. Makes 12-15 crackers. Nice to go with a salad or with butter and honey or cheese.

YEAST-RAISED PANCAKES OR WAFFLES

    1 tablespoon dried yeast or 1 cake yeast
    ¼ cup lukewarm water
    2 tablespoons honey
    1¼ cups milk (or use water and
        add ¼ cup dry milk to flour)
    2 eggs
    1 teaspoon sea salt or dulse
    2 tablespoons oil
    1 cup whole wheat flour
    ¼ cup soy flour
    ¼ cup wheat germ

Soak yeast in the water with the honey until bubbly, (Use *cool* liquid if you plan to keep overnight in refrigerator.) Combine milk (or water) in large bowl with beaten eggs and salt. Add yeast mixture and oil and, last of all, stir in dry ingredients which have been well mixed.

1 cup of buckwheat flour may be used in place of the wheat flour.

¼ teaspoon of maple extract or ½ teaspoon of vanilla will add to the delicious aroma when cooking. Bake on heated griddle or lightly oiled pan, until lightly browned on both sides.

For lighter cakes or waffles, let rise in a warm place for 20 minutes (or make the night before and store in the refrigerator). Serves 4-6.

WHEAT KERNEL PANCAKES (In blender)

Soak ½ cup whole wheat kernels in ½ cup water overnight. Next morning place 1 tablespoon dry yeast in ¼ cup warm water. Let soak 5 minutes. Drain wheat. Add enough milk to wheat to make 1¼ cups. Place soaked kernels and milk in blender and run 5 minutes. Then add:

   Yeast mixture
   3 egg yolks
   1 tablespoon molasses
   2 tablespoons melted butter or salad oil
   ¼ teaspoon sea salt
   3 tablespoons wheat germ

Blend enough to mix well. Transfer to a large bowl and let stand ten minutes in a warm place to rise. Then beat the 3 egg whites with a rotary beater until stiff, but not dry. Fold gently into the batter. Bake on a hot griddle or heavy frying pan.

Serve with honey, sorghum or fresh raw applesauce.* Serves 4.

COTTAGE CHEESE PANCAKES

   3 egg yolks
   ¾ cup cottage cheese
   ¼ cup whole-wheat pastry flour (or part may be soy flour or wheat germ)
   ½ teaspoon salt
   ½ teaspoon baking powder (optional)
   2 tablespoons salad oil
   3 egg whites, stiffly beaten
   1 tablespoon honey (optional)

Beat egg yolks till light and lemon colored. Sift together dry ingredients and add to egg yolks with cottage cheese. Add oil, and last of all egg whites, beaten stiff and gently folded in. One tablespoon honey may be added to egg whites after beating, if desired.

Bake on a medium hot griddle and serve with butter and honey. Serves 4.

RICE CAKES

2 eggs
1¾ cups cooked brown rice
3 tablespoons wheat germ
¼ teaspoon salt

Beat eggs slightly. Add rice, wheat germ and salt. Heat griddle to medium heat, 325°F. Add 1 tablespoon butter. Drop batter by tablespoons into hot butter. Flatten with back of spoon so cakes will be thin. When crisp and golden, about 4 minutes, turn cakes over and cook on other side. Serve with honey or sorghum. Serves 3-4.

VEGETABLE RICE

1 cup brown rice
2 cups water or broth
½ teaspoon sea salt

Toast rice in oven on a cookie sheet until golden brown. Transfer to a kettle. Add water and salt, cover and simmer 30 minutes, or until tender. Stir in

1 tablespoon butter
½ cup parsley, chopped
1 green onion, chopped
1 cup carrots, coarsely shredded

Cover and let stand 2 minutes, then serve. Serves 6.

DESSERTS

PRUNE GELATIN

1 cup dried prunes
1½ cups apple or pineapple juice
1 tablespoon plain gelatin
½ cup fruit juice or water, cold

Soak the prunes in the juice overnight. Pit and place in blender with juice. Blend to a mush. Remove to a bowl.

Sprinkle gelatin on the cold juice and mix. Melt over low heat, stirring. Add to the prune mixture. Stir. Pour into a mold or a bowl and chill. Serves 6.

Variations:

½ cup chopped nuts may be added
½ cup chopped apple is delicious also

Serve topped with yogurt or home-soured cream.

APPLE SNOW

1 cup applesauce (thick)
2 egg whites
1 tablespoon honey

Place in a deep bowl and beat with an egg beater until white and as thick as whipped cream. Serve piled into sherbet glasses. Top with finely ground nuts. (For younger children, omit nuts. Decorate with bits of persimmon or avocado). Serves 4.

INSTANT PUMPKIN PUDDING

2 cups raw pumpkin, include some seeds and
    pulp for flavor
2 raw eggs
¼ teaspoon kelp
½ teaspoon cinnamon
2 tablespoons honey
¼ orange or lemon or ½ banana

Place all in blender and liquefy. Add wheat germ to thicken if desired. Serve at once. Serves 4.

FRUIT WHIP

    1 cup juice, freshly made of apple, orange, grape,
        or home-canned grape or peach, or pear purée, or
        canned pineapple or grape juice
    1 banana
    1 sliced pear
    1 apple—if you do not have all three fruits, use three
        of any one kind

Buzz in blender. Divide the resulting thick fruit into four dessert dishes. Top with yogurt or whipped cream, if desired.

DATE CREAM DESSERT

Whip until stiff:

    1 pint whipping cream (certified raw if possible)

Fold in gently:

    2 tablespoons wheat germ
    1 cup chopped pecans
    ½ cup date sugar or honey
    2 cups chopped dates
    2 tablespoons orange or pineapple juice

Chill and serve. Serves 10-12.

DATE ICE CREAM

Soak ½ cup dates in 1 cup milk several hours or overnight. Place in blender and add:

    1 cup cream
    1 teaspoon vanilla
    Dash of sea salt

Cover and run machine until thoroughly blended. Put in freezing tray and freeze. For smoother dessert, remove once and blend or beat smooth. Return to tray and finish freezing. Serves 4.

MELON COMPOTE WITH AVOCADO CREAM DRESSING

One hour before use, place—
- 1 avocado in blender, add:
- 1½ cups sour cream or yogurt
- 2 tablespoons lemon juice
- 2 tablespoons honey

Beat 2 minutes or until smooth. Serve over fresh melons. Use honeydew, watermelon, cantaloupe—cubed or in balls. Spoon avocado dressing over all. Makes about 2 cups of dressing.

CAROB SOUFFLE PUDDING

Soften 2 tablespoons (or packages) of plain gelatin in ½ cup of milk for 5 minutes. Then melt, over low heat, stirring constantly. Remove from the stove. In ice-cold blender bowl, place the following:

- 1 egg or 2 egg yolks
- 1 medium banana, in large slices
- 1 teaspoon sea salt or dulse
- ½ cup carob powder
- 1 teaspoon vanilla
- 4 tablespoons honey
- 2 cups milk

Blend well and add gelatin mixture from above. Chill until syrupy. Meanwhile, whip one cup of cream in a chilled, 2-quart bowl. Fold carob mixture gently into cream, and pour into casserole or glass baking dish. Sprinkle chopped cashews or almonds over the top and chill until firm. Cut in squares to serve, or scoop up with large spoon. Serves 10-12.

APPLESAUCE (RAW)

In blender place:

- 3 tablespoons pineapple juice or yogurt
- 1 teaspoon cinnamon

Add gradually: 3 large apples—if organically grown do not peel or core. Wash, quarter, and cut in small pieces. Gradually add to blender, a small amount at a time. Scrape down sides with rubber spatula. Sweeten to taste with 2 or 3 tablespoons honey or date sugar and add ½ teaspoon vanilla or a sliver of orange rind for flavor. Remove from blender and chill in a covered jar if not to be used at once.

Variation: Ginger pears—make as above, using 1 teaspoon fresh chopped ginger root in place of cinnamon, and 5 medium pears, sliced, in place of apples.

Serve as pancake topping. For dessert, pile into sherbet glass, spoon whipped cream over the top and sprinkle with chopped nuts. Serves 4.

QUICK ORANGE MARMALADE

1 cup·honey placed in blender with
2 whole oranges, cut in pieces (do not use rinds of commercially grown fruit)
4 orange rinds

Blend all together well.

Variation: Add ¼ cup fresh mint leaves before blending.

Serve on hot pancakes, made with soy or whole-grain flours, hot rolls, custard, or use to top ice cream. Makes 1½ pints of marmalade.

APPLE-DATE BUTTER

1 large apple, peeled and seeded, cut in pieces
½ cup apple juice (or pineapple juice)
12 large dates, pitted

Blend together the apple and the juice. Begin adding dates, 3 or 4 at a time. Cover and blend. Keep adding dates until the mixture is smooth and as thick as you wish. One-half cup sunflower seeds may be added for a crunchy spread. Good on apple slices, banana rounds, or whole-grain bread. Keep any unused portion in the refrigerator. Makes about 1½ cups of apple-date butter.

BANANA-APRICOT SHERBET

    2 cups apricot purée (or fresh apricots)
    2 bananas
    1 cup orange juice
    ½ cup cream or yogurt
    Honey to taste

Place all ingredients in the blender and run until smooth. Pour into two ice-cube trays or one large freezing tray. Freeze until hard at about ¼ inch around the edges. Scrape into a large bowl and beat until smooth and fluffy. Return to freezer and freeze until firm. Makes 1 quart of sherbet.

Variations: Use peaches in place of apricots and apple juice instead of orange juice. Yogurt gives a tart fruity taste, while cream makes a richer product. ½ cup almond butter or other nut butter may be used in place of the cream or yogurt for a rich, nutty ice cream.

FRESH STRAWBERRY PIE

Crumb crust:

    1 cup honey graham cracker crumbs
    ½ cup wheat germ
    ¼ cup sesame seeds or finely chopped nuts
    ¼ teaspoon nutmeg
    ⅓ cup butter, melted

Crush crackers in a tea towel with rolling pin or crumb a few at a time in blender. Combine crumbs, wheat germ, sesame seeds, nutmeg and melted butter. Mix thoroughly. Press evenly over bottom and up the sides of a 9-inch pie pan. Freeze until needed.

Filling:

    2 pints strawberries
    1½ cups apple or pineapple juice
    2 tablespoons arrowroot
    ¼ cup honey

Wash and hull berries. Heat 1¼ cups juice in a 1½ quart saucepan. Mix arrowroot with reserved juice and add to boiling juice. Cook over medium heat until thick and clear. Remove from heat and stir in honey and 1 cup strawberries, sliced. Cover and let set at room temperature till cool.

Remove crust from freezer. Fill with remaining berries, the larger ones sliced. Pour the sauce over the berries and return to freezer for a few moments. Serve with whipped cream. Serves 6.

CARROT CAKE

    4 eggs
    2 teaspoons vanilla
    1 teaspoon dry yeast soaked in 1 tablespoon
        lukewarm pineapple juice
    4 medium carrots, cut in small pieces
    2½ cups wholewheat pastry flour or 2 cups
        wholewheat pastry flour, ¼ cup soy flour
        and ¼ cup wheat germ
    1 teaspoon sea salt
    2 teaspoons cinnamon
    1 tablespoon carob powder
    2 teaspoons baking powder (buy at Health Food store)
    1 cup chopped nuts
    1 cup chopped dates or raisins
    1 cup crushed pineapple (well drained)
    1 cup oil
    1 cup thick honey)   or you may use 2 cups
    1 cup date sugar)   yellow D brown sugar
    Grated rind from one orange
    Cream cheese or whipping cream

Break eggs into blender bowl. Add vanilla and soaked yeast and juice. Blend 30 seconds. Begin adding carrot pieces, blending after each 4 or 5 pieces until material in blender reaches the 3½ cup mark. Place all dry ingredients in a bowl. Add fruit and nuts. Make a well in the center, pour in the oil, add honey and date sugar (or brown sugar). Mix together, then add carrots and eggs from blender and grated rind. Mix all ingredients together with a wooden spoon until thoroughly blended. Bake in a greased and floured 9 x 13 inch baking dish or a tube pan at 350°F. for about 45 minutes or until golden brown. Frost with cream cheese sweetened with honey or use whipped cream topping (see index). This cake is actually better the second day if there is any left.

APPLE CRISP

6 apples, washed and cored
1 cup date sugar or yellow D sugar
½ teaspoon sea salt
1 teaspoon cinnamon
½ cup butter
½ cup wholewheat pastry flour or other
   whole-grain flour
¼ cup wheat germ

Slice apples thin and place in a well buttered baking dish. Mix all other ingredients in a bowl. Crumble with fingers until well mixed. Spread over apples and bake in a 350°F. oven for about 40 minutes. Serves 6.

DATE NUT TORTE

8 egg whites (left over from making banana
   pudding or mayonnaise) or
4 egg yolks
4 egg whites
½ cup honey
1 cup chopped dates
1 cup chopped nuts
1 teaspoon vanilla
½ teaspoon sea salt
¼ cup wheat germ
¼ cup soy flour or rice polishings

Beat egg whites until stiff but not dry, or beat 4 egg yolks, add honey and beat well to blend. Stir in vanilla and dates. Fold in salt, wheat germ and flour and last of all, gently fold in 1 cup chopped nuts or a mixture of seeds and nuts. (Pulp left from making nut milk will be fine for this recipe.) If you have used egg yolks, now fold in the stiffly beaten whites. Pour into buttered pan (8½ x 11 inches) and bake at 350°F. for about 20 minutes. When cool cut in squares and serve with whipped cream. For the lunch box it is good served plain.

SPICY PEANUT BUTTER PUDDING

½ cup soft butter
½ cup peanut butter (from health food store or
    dairy case at your market)
2 eggs, beaten
⅓ cup honey
Grated rind and juice of 1 lemon
¾ cup wholewheat pastry flour
¼ cup soy flour or wheat germ (if wheat germ,
    mix with lemon rind to add)
¼ teaspoon sea salt
¼ teaspoon **each** nutmeg and allspice
⅛ teaspoon baking powder
⅛ teaspoon cloves, ground
1 cup chopped dates or raisins
1 cup shredded carrot—raw
1 cup chopped nuts
½ cup crushed pineapple—drained

Cream butter; blend in peanut butter. Beat in eggs, honey, lemon rind and juice. Add sifted dry ingredients and mix well. Stir in dates or raisins, carrots, nuts, and pineapple. Pack into 8 well oiled custard cups (5 or 6 oz.). Set in pan of hot water and bake in a moderate (350°F.) oven for 55 to 60 minutes. Unmold into serving dishes and serve warm with whipped cream topping.

WHIPPED CREAM TOPPING

½ cup whipping cream
⅛ cup top milk
2 tablespoons dry skim milk powder, **not** instant
2 tablespoons honey
1 teaspoon vanilla

Beat cream until fairly thick, add milk, dry milk and continue beating. Add honey and vanilla. Chill until served.

ENTREES

BAKED HEART WITH DRESSING

Steam until tender, one medium beef or two small veal hearts. Remove fat and sinew. Dice into ½-inch cubes. Place a layer of the dressing in a baking pan. Spread over it a layer of diced heart. Repeat layers, ending with a layer of dressing and bake at 300°F. until golden brown. Serve with a brown gravy made from the broth in which the heart was cooked.

CORNBREAD DRESSING

    3 tablespoons oil
    1 onion, chopped
    2 stalks celery and tops, chopped
    1 cup dry cornbread crumbs
    ½ cup wholewheat bread crumbs
    ¼ cup wheat germ
    3 tablespoons parsley, chopped
    1 tablespoon sea salt or dulse
    ½ teaspoon sage
    ½ teaspoon thyme
    ½ teaspoon marjoram
    2 eggs, beaten
    1 cup hot turkey or chicken stock
    ½ cup chopped nuts

Heat oil; saute onion and celery; add to crumbs, wheat germ, parsley and spices. Mix in beaten eggs and gradually add hot stock and nuts. Makes 8 servings.

NOTE: This dressing may be used to stuff a five-pound chicken. Ground beef may be used instead of the diced heart. Use the beef *raw* and proceed as directed.

ORIENTAL CHICKEN

In electric stainless steel fry-pan place 1 tablespoon salad oil. Set thermostat at 250° to 300°. When warm add 2 boned chicken breasts, cut in small pieces, stir and fry until covered all over with oil. Push to one side and

Add:

    ½ cup celery, sliced
    ¼ cup sweet red peppers, sliced
    ¼ cup onion, chopped
    1 cup mung bean sprouts
    ¼ cup sugar pod peas—optional
    ¼ cup sliced mushrooms

Stir well and cook 5 minutes, covered. Turn off fire; season with 1 tablespoon (or more) soy sauce, 1 teaspoon seasoned salt, 1 teaspoon herbed seasoning. Cover a few moments. Serve with steamed brown rice. Serves 4.

Variation: 1 cup diced beef or veal heart may be used in the above recipe. Remove fat and sinew. Cut into one-half inch cubes. Proceed as directed. ¼ teaspoon dried sage may be added to the seasoning. Some like the liquid thickened with 1 teaspoon arrowroot dissolved in 2 tablespoons broth or water. Adjust the seasonings and serve over steamed brown rice.

STEAMED BROWN RICE

2 cups water
1 cup short-grain brown rice
1 teaspoon sea salt

Soak rice in water for one-half hour or longer in a cool place. Bring to a boil in covered pan over medium heat. Immediately lower heat to below boiling and steam gently about 45 minutes or until tender and water is evaporated. Serves 4.

STEAMED SOYBEANS

1 cup soybeans
2 cups water

Soak for twenty-four hours in a cool place, then add:

1 small onion, chopped
½ teaspoon sea salt
Juice of 1 lemon

Simmer over a very low fire or in the top of a double boiler for four or five hours. They are now ready to eat or to use in other dishes. Serves 4.

ALMOND SOY CASSEROLE

1 cup cooked or canned soybeans, mashed
1 cup very finely ground almonds
4 tablespoons grated carrots
2 tablespoons celery, diced
2 tablespoons tomato purée

Bake in a well oiled glass baking dish for about 25 minutes at 350°F. Makes 4 servings.

SALAD DRESSINGS

COUNTRY GARDEN SALAD DRESSING

3 ripe tomatoes, cut up
1 cup cabbage, in pieces
1 green onion
2 eggs, or 4 egg yolks
¼ cup yogurt
2 tablespoons salad oil
1 teaspoon sea salt or dulse
¼ teaspoon herbed seasoning

Place all in blender and run until smooth. Chill before serving. A colorful dressing for a green salad. Add chopped hard-cooked eggs or soaked almonds for a light lunch or supper. Makes about 2 cups of dressing.

PINEAPPLE SALAD DRESSING

2 eggs
2 tablespoons arrowroot
1 cup pineapple juice, unsweetened
¼ cup lemon juice
⅓ cup honey
½ cup whipping cream

Beat eggs, add arrowroot and pineapple juice. Cook in top of double boiler over boiling water until the mixture thickens, stirring constantly. Remove from heat. Add lemon juice and honey. Chill. Add whipped cream. Serve over fruit salads. Makes about 2¼ cups of dressing.

MAYONNAISE

2 fresh fertile eggs or 4 egg yolks
1 teaspoon sea salt or dulse
½ teaspoon paprika
Dash of herbed seasoning

Beat well, then add:
1 tablespoon boiling water

Beat again. Now slowly add—with the beater on low:
1½ cups cold pressed salad oil

When well blended, add:
3 tablespoons cider vinegar or lemon juice
and mix well.

Makes 2¼ cups of mayonnaise.

VARIATIONS:

YOGURT DRESSING

½ cup mayonnaise
1 cup yogurt
¼ teaspoon herbed seasoning
½ teaspoon sea salt
1 tablespoon chopped parsley
⅛ teaspoon curry powder

Mix well and chill overnight to blend the flavors.
Makes 1¼ cups of dressing.

BEET MAYONNAISE

⅓ cup mayonnaise
⅓ cup sour cream or yogurt
1 cup shredded raw beets, or freshly cooked beets

Mix thoroughly and serve over lettuce wedges, or
chilled cucumber slices. Makes 1½ cups of mayonnaise.

BLEU CHEESE DRESSING

½ cup mayonnaise
½ cup yogurt or sour cream
1 oz. bleu cheese, crumbled
1 teaspoon chopped onion (optional)

Makes 1 cup of dressing.

THOUSAND ISLAND DRESSING

1 cup mayonnaise
1/4 cup thick tomato purée
1/2 cup yogurt or sour cream
1/4 cup chopped ripe olives
1 egg, hardboiled, chopped
1 tablespoon parsley, chopped.

Makes 2 cups of dressing.

CREAMY FRENCH DRESSING

Just blend
1 cup of your favorite French dressing with
1/2 cup of mayonnaise

Makes 1½ cups of dressing.

CASHEW MAYONNAISE

Place in blender bowl:

1/2 cup raw cashews
1 teaspoon dulse or kelp
1/2 teaspoon paprika
Garlic or onion, to taste, or use herbed seasoning
1 cup water

Blend well, then add slowly—
1 cup salad oil
Run until smooth, then pour in while running
Juice of 2 lemons or 2 tablespoons cider vinegar

Delicious with either fruit or vegetable salad. Try it with potatoes steamed in jackets, peeled and cubed. Add diced celery, green and red peppers, herbs and dressing. Makes about 2¼ cups of mayonnaise.

TANGY SALAD DRESSING

2/3 cup salad oil
1/3 cup cider vinegar or lemon juice
2 tablespoons water or pineapple juice
2 teaspoons soy sauce
1 teaspoon honey (optional)
1/2 teaspoon sea salt or dulse
3/4 teaspoon herbed seasoning
1/2 teaspoon dried sweet basil

Shake all together well. If you enjoy garlic, place 1 garlic bud in dressing overnight. Remove the next day. Chill until ready to serve. Makes about 1 cup of dressing.

DRESSING FOR GREEN BEAN or MIXED BEAN SALAD

- 3 tablespoons cider vinegar
- 3 tablespoons salad oil
- ½ cup chicken stock (see note)
- 1 teaspoon sea salt
- 1 teaspoon fresh dill weed, chopped, or
- 1 tablespoon fresh parsley, or
- ½ teaspoon dried parsley
- ½ teaspoon herbed seasoning

Beat with a whisk the vinegar, oil, chicken stock, salt and seasonings. Stir in the parsley and dill. Set aside to blend. Chill. Can be made in a blender.

NOTE: Poach chicken breasts or thighs for salad. Save stock.

SALADS

GREEN BEAN SALAD

Marinate in dressing for one hour, or overnight,

- ½ pound freshly cooked green beans
- 2½ red sweet peppers, diced
- 1 medium onion, diced

Serves 6.

MIXED BEAN SALAD

1 cup each green beans, kidney beans and garbanzos—Marinate as above. If desired, 1 onion, diced, may be added. Serves 6.

CHEESE AND MUSHROOM SALAD

2 cups salad greens—washed, crisped and torn into
    bite-sized pieces
½ cup sprouts (any kind) chopped
¼ cup marinated mushrooms
2 medium tomatoes, sliced
¼ lb. Swiss cheese grated
½ lemon peel, grated

Mix greens, sprouts and mushrooms. Toss with just
enough dressing to moisten well. Add sliced tomatoes
and top generously with grated lemon and shredded
cheese. Serves 6.

MARINATED MUSHROOMS

¼ lb. tiny raw button mushrooms or large mush-
    rooms, sliced

Cover with tangy salad dressing and keep chilled in
jar until needed. When ready to serve, drain dressing off
in sieve and return dressing to bottle. Toss mushrooms
with green salad.

MOLDED FRUIT SALAD

1 envelope unflavored gelatin
¼ cup apple juice
2 tablespoons raw honey
1 tablespoon fresh lemon juice
1 teaspoon vanilla extract
1¼ cups raw buttermilk (or ¾ c. nut milk blended
    with ½ cup yogurt)
1½ cups fresh fruit, cut up (mixed apples, grapes,
    peaches, cherries, bananas)
½ cup chopped nuts

Soak gelatin in the apple juice—place over low heat
and stir until melted. Add honey, lemon juice, vanilla
and buttermilk or yogurt and nut milk. Chill until mixture begins to thicken. Fold in the fruit mixture and
nuts. Chill until firm, at least 4 hours, unmold on
chilled platter and decorate with pieces of fruit and
parsley. Serves 6.

ROSY GLOW SALAD

½ cup grated raw beets (peeled)
⅔ cup celery, diced
2 red apples, diced (do not peel, if organically
    grown)

DRESSING

2 tablespoon salad oil
1 tablespoon cider vinegar or lemon juice
Sprinkle of nutmeg

Blend all ingredients well (double recipe will work
well in the blender), mix into salad and let stand 5
minutes before serving. Serves 4-6.

CARROT-COCONUT-DATE SALAD

Mix:

2 cups grated carrots
½ cup grated coconut
1 cup crushed unsweetened pineapple
½ cup diced dates or raisins

Serve on bed of green lettuce with sour cream or
whipped cream dressing—honey sweetened. Serves 6.

GUACAMOLE

2 good-sized avocados, ripe enough to mash
2 tablespoons lemon juice
2 tablespoons very finely chopped onion
½ teaspoon sea salt
½ clove garlic (rub mixing bowl with it and discard)
1 ripe tomato, peeled, seeded and chopped

Cut avocados in half. Tap the seed with the sharp
edge of a knife, so it sticks in the seed. Twist the knife
and lift out the seed. Peel avocado and mash with a fork
or place in blender. Add remaining ingredients, blending well.

For grown ups you may wish to add 1 or 2 chopped
"green chiles"—the kind that are sold in cans as "peeled
green chiles." Remove seeds and wash under running

water carefully, unless you like your food very hot. Or you may flavor with a bit of cumin powder or more garlic. This is a positively addictive spread or dip. Use raw vegetables or tortillas for dippers. Or spread over medium cucumbers halved lengthwise and top with sour cream and chopped fresh parsley. Omit the chopped tomato and heap on top of huge tomato slices. Spoon onto whole-wheat toast or warmed tortillas, sprinkle with cheese and pop under the broiler just long enough to melt the cheese. May also be used as dressing for a tossed green salad. Serves 4.

RAW VEGETABLE SALAD

    1 cucumber, sliced
    ½ cup cabbage, chopped
    1 carrot, thinly sliced
    1 green onion in 1 inch slices
    1 zucchini, cut in half, then sliced in
        ½ inch pieces
    ¼ cup parsley, chopped
    ¼ cup celery, sliced
    ¼ cup grated cheddar cheese
    2 young beets, shredded

Mix all but beets very lightly with an oil-vinegar dressing. Garnish each serving with the shredded beet. Serves 4.

SAUERKRAUT SALAD

    2 cups **raw** sauerkraut
    1 cup pineapple juice, unsweetened
    ½ cup salad oil
    ¼ cup cider vinegar
    2 tablespoons honey
    1 cup apple, diced, unpared
    ½ cup celery, sliced
    1 large red or green sweet pepper, diced

Wash sauerkraut; drain well and marinate in the pineapple juice overnight. At serving time, drain the pineapple juice, reserving ¼ cup for the dressing. In serving bowl place the reserved juice, oil, vinegar and honey; mix well. Add sauerkraut, apple, celery and peppers. Toss and serve chilled. Serves 6.

SPROUT SALAD

1 cup sprouts, any kind
1/4 cup sugar peas—in the pod
1/2 cup carrot, shredded
1/4 cup celery, shredded

Chop sprouts and break peas in small pieces. Mix with other vegetables and serve. Serves 4.

WALDORF SALAD WITH TURKEY

1/2 cup mayonnaise
1/4 cup pineapple juice
1/4 cup yogurt
1 tablespoon lemon juice
2 teaspoons sea salt
2 red apples, unpeeled
1 golden delicious apple, unpeeled
1/2 cup celery, sliced
1/2 cup pineapple, crushed, unsweetened
1/2 cup walnuts or pecans, broken
1 1/2 cups diced cooked turkey or chicken
Chopped parsley

Mix mayonnaise, pineapple juice, yogurt, lemon juice and salt. Core and dice apples into the dressing, turning to cover thoroughly and prevent darkening. Add celery, pineapple, nuts and turkey; toss lightly. Trim with chopped parsley. Serves 6.

RAINBOW SALAD PLATE

1 parsnip, shredded
1 zucchini, shredded
1 carrot, shredded
1 beet, shredded

Place vegetables in separate piles around edge of a large salad platter. Place a small bowl with tangy salad dressing or bleu cheese dressing in the center. Garnish with green pepper rings filled with radishes. Serves 4.

OLIVE COLE SLAW

2 cups cabbage, shredded
½ cup carrot, shredded
½ cup red or green sweet peppers
½ cup chopped black olives

Mix lightly together and dress with a mixture of mayonnaise and yogurt. Serves 4.

PEARS AND CHEESE SALAD

8 pear halves, home-canned if possible
½ cup cream, whipped
1 teaspoon honey
1 teaspoon grated lemon rind
½ cup grated cheddar cheese

Place two pear halves, round side up, on each salad plate. Frost each half with cream mixed with honey and lemon rind. Sprinkle the cheese over the top. 4 servings.

CABBAGE-APPLE SALAD

1 cup cabbage, shredded
1 cup red apple with peel (if organic), chopped
½ cup pecans, chopped
¼ cup yogurt
¼ cup pineapple juice, unsweetened
1 tablespoon lemon juice
1 teaspoon honey
½ cup seedless grapes

Mix together cabbage, apple and pecans. Stir together the yogurt, pineapple juice, lemon juice and honey. Gently blend into salad. Garnish with grapes. Serves 4.

BANANAS WITH CREAM CHEESE DRESSING

2 egg yolks
2 tablespoons honey
1 tablespoon orange juice
½ teaspoon vanilla
1 8 oz. package cream cheese, softened
3 tablespoons yogurt
3 bananas
chopped nuts

Beat egg yolks, honey, orange juice and vanilla until thick and lemon-colored. Gradually beat in cream cheese till smooth and fluffy. Add yogurt and chill. Serve over sliced bananas—sprinkle with chopped nuts. Serves 4.

FRUIT SALAD WITH STRAWBERRY SAUCE

    2 oranges
    1 banana
    1 peach
    1 papaya, cut in one-inch cubes
    1 cup fresh grapes, seedless
    1 cup fresh raspberries or blueberries

Section the oranges over a shallow bowl to catch the juice. Slice the banana and peach into the juice. Turn to coat all sides of the fruit. Add papaya and grapes; chill. Arrange fruits on romaine or other lettuce in serving bowl. Add the berries. Serve with strawberry sauce.

SAUCES

STRAWBERRY SAUCE

    1 cup strawberries
    ¼ cup pineapple juice
    2 teaspoons gelatin
    ¼ cup yogurt

Soak the gelatin in juice for a few moments, in a small kettle. Melt over low heat, stirring constantly. Place strawberries in blender. Blend one minute, add melted gelatin and yogurt. Buzz again. Chill until serving time. Serves 6-8.

DILL FISH SAUCE

1 cup mayonnaise
½ cup yogurt
½ cup buttermilk (or use 1 cup yogurt in all)
¼ teaspoon sea salt
¼ teaspoon herbed seasoning
1 teaspoon fresh dill weed, finely chopped (when not in season use dill seed or omit salt and use dill salt)
1 tablespoon chopped ripe olives (optional)

Let set overnight in the refrigerator for the flavors to blend. Serve with oven-baked or broiled fish fillets. Serves 6.

QUICK CREAM SAUCE

Place in saucepan over low heat

1 cup milk
3 slices wholewheat bread

Simmer, stirring constantly, until thickened. Add sea salt to taste. Makes 1½ cups of sauce.

CHEESE SAUCE

Cheese sauce: add 1 cup grated cheese to quick cream sauce after removing from the heat, 1 teaspoon herbed seasoning and ¼ teaspoon paprika. Makes 1¾ cups of sauce.

PARSLEY SAUCE

¼ medium onion
1 clove garlic
¼ cup wholewheat bread crumbs
¼ cup salad oil—part **olive** if desired
Juice of 1 lemon
1 bunch of parsley with the stems removed
1 hard boiled egg, chopped

Slice onion into blender, add garlic, crumbs, oil and lemon. Blend until smooth. Start adding parsley a little at a time. Continue blending until all is blended into the sauce. Remove from blender to bowl and combine with chopped egg.

Good over large slices of chilled tomatoes, sliced fresh zucchini or steamed green beans.

This sauce can be made without a blender. Soak the bread crumbs in the oil. Smash the garlic with the flat side of your chef's knife and add to bread and oil. Add the lemon. On chopping board, chop parsley very fine, until it is like green velvet. Blend into the bread mixture. Add chopped egg last. Serves 4.

KITCHEN-MADE CATSUP

1 #2½ can tomato purée or concentrate
3 6 oz. cans tomato paste
½ cup cider vinegar (or tarragon vinegar)
4 tablespoons honey (may use ½ molasses)
½ teaspoon cloves
1½ teaspoons allspice
3 teaspoons cinnamon
1 tablespoon salt or to taste
¼ teaspoon each onion, celery and garlic salt
    or herbed seasonings

Mix all ingredients together and pour into sterilized pint jars. Chill at once and place in refrigerator till used.

Commercial varieties of catsup are made with quantities of sugar as well as undesirable preservatives. For the *child*, use even homemade catsup in moderation. Makes about 3 pints.

SOUPS

VEGETABLE SOUP

(Begin preparation the day before you wish to serve this soup.)

½ cup dried lima beans, pinto beans, lentils or other legumes
4 or 5 marrow bones from organically grown beef
1 large shank or other soup bones
4 tablespoons butter
2 carrots, sliced
1 large onion, diced
¼ cup green pepper, diced
2 or 3 stalks celery, sliced
1 tablespoon cider vinegar—add to soup with bones
1 teaspoon sea salt
thyme, bay leaf, savory (herbs to season)
1 large tomato

In season use:

1 ear corn on the cob, sliced in 4 pieces (use cob for flavor)
15 or so washed pods from green peas (reserve peas for soup at later stage)

Soak the beans overnight in 6 cups of cold water. (For meatless soup, use 1 cup beans.) Bring to a boil, skim and set to simmer slowly in a large stainless-steel kettle. Use the water in which they were soaked to cook them in, as it will contain valuable minerals. Remove the marrow from inside the marrow bones, and place in the refrigerator to add later. Brown the bones in butter and add to the simmering beans with the other soup bones. Bring to a boil again and skim if necessary. Turn down the fire and add vegetables, seasonings and herbs. Add water to cover and simmer over a very low fire for at least three hours (four or five hours will make a move flavorful stock). Any clean left-over salad greens or vegetables from previous meals may be used in this broth; add with the other vegetables. Cool to room temperature and chill in refrigerator until fat rises to top and can be lifted off. Strain the broth. This is now ready to use or to store in the freezer or refrigerator. Makes 2 quarts of broth.

For immediate serving, place 4 cups of broth in a large pot. Add:

> 2 cups diced carrots
> 1 large onion, diced
> ½ green pepper, diced
> 3 stalks celery, sliced
> 1 turnip or 1 rutabaga, diced

Bring to a boil, then simmer very slowly for 10 minutes. Now add:

> ½ cup diced potato or corn cut from the cob
> 1 large tomato, sliced
> ½ cup shredded cabbage

Cook three minutes longer. Then add:

> ½ cup fresh or frozen green peas
> ½ cup fresh parsley, chopped
> ¼ cup fresh okra, sliced

Cook gently just a few minutes and add the reserved bone marrow. Heat just long enough to melt marrow into the soup. Serve at once in warm bowls with 1 tablespoon diced raw avocado in each bowl, or fresh chives on top. Makes 6 generous servings.

There are as many variations of this soup as there are cooks. The beans or lentils may be cooked separately in a small pan and added to the broth with the last part of the vegetables. Use the broth they were cooked in also. Any vegetable that you enjoy may be used; just remember to add the hardest ones first—the ones requiring little or no cooking at the last minute.

For raw soup: Place 1 cup broth in your blender; add any raw vegetables used above in ½ cup amounts. Blend and serve at once. You will like it, and it may be served to your children over one year of age.

GAZPACHO—SPANISH SALAD SOUP

½ cup tomato juice (home-canned or pressed raw
    from fresh tomatoes)
2 medium tomatoes (ripe)
¼ green pepper
¼ small onion or three green onions
½ cucumber
2 tablespoons fresh parsley
Sprig of fresh dill, when in season
1 tablespoon cider vinegar
½ teaspoon sea salt or dulse
½ teaspoon herbed seasoning
¼ fresh garlic clove, or garlic salt

Place juice in blender. Cut tomatoes in quarters, slice peppers, onion or green onions and cucumbers. Blend all for three seconds. Chill for two hours or more. Serve with a dab of sour cream on top (see page 105), or add diced avocado. Serves 4.

To make this a soup of great variety, add any of the following:

1 raw egg yolk, ½ cup coarsely chopped tomato, 1 cup chicken broth, 1 cup clam broth, 1 tablespoon sour cream; mix with the other ingredients.

PUMPKIN SOUP

(Peel pumpkin, remove strings and seeds—dice in blender.)

1 cup prepared pumpkin
1 cup chicken broth (may be prepared with broth
    powder from health food store)
¼ teaspoon paprika
½ teaspoon herbed seasoning
½ teaspoon kelp or dulse
¼ teaspoon nutmeg

Blend until smooth and thick. Then add:

1 more cup chicken broth
1 cup creamy milk or nut milk

Buzz one minute. Heat gently to serving temperature, adjust seasoning and serve in warm bowls. Serves 4.

GREEN VEGETABLE SOUP

You will need 2 cups vegetable broth (vegetable cooking water or bone broth may be used, plus broth powder). Place in blender bowl ½ cup of the broth and herbs to season, such as 1 mint leaf, sprig of marjoram, rosemary, savory, or your own favorites.

    1 cup asparagus, sliced
    ½ cup parsley
    2 small comfrey leaves
    ¼ cup watercress or fresh peas
    ½ cup raw spinach or New Zealand spinach
    ¼ cup green onions or chives
    You may substitute any green vegetables you enjoy.

Gradually blend in more broth with the vegetables, making it as thick or thin as you like. Season with herbed seasonings such as Yerba Encanta or Sea Zun and dulse or kelp. Gently warm to just serving temperature. Serve in warm bowls. Makes 4 servings.

For a creamy variation, add: 1 large ear of corn, cut from cob. Blend, warm and serve.

LEBANESE LENTIL SOUP

    1 cup lentils
    2 tablespoons oil or butter
    1 cup celery, chopped
    1 cup carrots, diced
    1 medium onion, chopped
    3 cups water or soup stock
    1 teaspoon sea salt or dulse
    2 tablespoons fresh lemon juice

Soak lentils in 3 cups of water or soup stock water overnight or for a few hours. Place oil in frying pan and add celery, carrots, and onions. Sauté, stirring constantly for a few minutes to release the flavors. Add vegetables and sea salt or dulse to lentils in cooking pot. Bring to boil; lower heat at once and simmer below the boiling point until tender, about 45 to 50 minutes. Add the lemon juice just before serving. Serves 4.

If you have sprouted lentils, ¼ cup may be finely

chopped and added with the lemon juice for additional flavor and nutrients.

SOYBEAN SOUP

½ cup celery, chopped
1 cup carrots, diced (2 medium)
1 medium onion, chopped
½ red or green sweet pepper
2 cups broth or water
1 teaspoon kelp or sea salt
1 cup cooked soybeans, mashed
2 fresh tomatoes, chopped or
1 cup tomatoes, cooked or canned
1 tablespoon parsley

Simmer the celery, carrots, onion and pepper gently in the seasoned broth or water for 10 to 15 minutes. Add the cooked soybeans and chopped tomato. Heat to serving temperature and serve in warm bowls. Sprinkle chopped parsley on top. Serves 4.

RAW MUSHROOM CREAM SOUP

¾ cup onion, chopped
2 cups celery, chopped
2 tablespoons butter or oil
1¼ cups chicken broth
1½ tablespoons arrowroot
6 large mushrooms or equivalent small ones
¼ cup cream, raw if possible
½ teaspoon each: sea salt, herbed seasoning and nutmeg

Sauté onions and celery in butter very slowly, until tender. Add 1 cup chicken broth and bring to boil. Thicken with arrowroot dissolved in ¼ cup broth. Stir until thick and clear. Wash mushrooms; slice into blender. Carefully pour in hot soup, cover and blend 2 minutes. Add cream and serve. Garnish with sliced mushroom and a dash of paprika. Serves 4.

JELLIED BEET BORSCHT

4 raw beets—if tender and new, scrub well and cut in small pieces—use medium-size beets
1 cup apple or pineapple juice or beet juice

Place juice in blender, add beets and buzz until very fine. If time permits, cover lightly and let set at room temperature 12 to 24 hours to develop the delicious cidery lactic acid. Add:

    3 tablespoons (or less) tupelo honey
    4 tablespoons yogurt or home-soured cream
    3 tablespoons lemon juice or cider vinegar
    ¼ teaspoon each: mace, cardomom and
        sea salt or purple dulse

In small pot, place ¼ cup apple or pineapple juice. Add 2 tablespoons plain gelatin, soak 5 minutes. Melt over low heat, stirring constantly. Add to beet mixture with 3 additional cups juice. Chill. Frost with sour cream or yogurt and cut in squares to serve. 9 to 12 servings.

Gelatin may be omitted. Chill, and serve as a refreshing soup with a spoonful of sour cream on top.

CASHEW-BEET BORSCHT

    1 cup pineapple juice
    4 medium beets—prepared as above
    1 cup cashew nuts or
    3 tablespoons Tahini
    1 cup yogurt
    Juice of 1 lemon

Place pineapple juice in blender, add beets, and blend. Then add other ingredients (except lemon juice) and blend once more. Add lemon juice and serve at once. Serves 4.

FISH CHOWDER

2 tablespoons butter
½ cup onion, chopped
½ cup celery, chopped
½ bay leaf, finely crumbled
¼ teaspoon fresh or dried dill weed (optional)
1 teaspoon sea salt or dulse
1½ cups water
2 cups potatoes, diced
1 pound fish, cut in small pieces
2 cups rich milk (or ½ milk, ½ cream)
¼ cup parsley, chopped
paprika

Melt butter in heavy kettle; add onions and sauté until tender. Add celery, bay leaf and seasonings; mix well with onions and cook one minute. Add water, potatoes and fish. Cover and simmer very gently until potatoes are tender, 15 to 20 minutes. Add cream and milk; heat to serving temperature and serve in warm bowls. Garnish with parsley and dust with paprika. Fish may be cod, halibut, haddock, bass, snapper, bonita, or other local varieties; or try this with scallops. Makes 4 to 6 servings.

SPREADS

RAW BUTTER OIL SPREAD

Let 1 pound of raw butter (if raw is not available, use other) set at room temperature until it is soft enough to stir. Slowly add and stir in with a spoon: 1½ cups cold-pressed salad oil and 1 teaspoon powdered lecithin. A mixture of two kinds of oils makes a fine-flavored product. Place in covered bowls in refrigerator until needed.

ALMOND BUTTER

Grind ½ pound of unroasted almonds through a food chopper two or three times, using the finest plate. When the nuts are fine enough to be like butter, add:

    1 tablespoon salad oil
    ½ teaspoon sea salt

Mix well, pack into jars, and close tightly.

MIXED NUT AND SEED BUTTER

    ½ cup almonds
    ½ cup cashews
    ½ cup filberts
    ¼ cup each of sesame seed, sunflower seed, pumpkin
        seed and flax seed

Grind in a little nut mill or in your blender (one variety at a time) and pour into a mixing bowl. Slowly add fresh salad oil—just enough to make a soft nut butter. Spread on slices of banana or apple; roll up in lettuce leaves for finger salad; spread on slices of raw turnip or potato for an after-school snack. May be mixed with chopped, organically-grown raisins and spread on fruit slices or whole-grain bread.

PARTY CHEESE SPREAD

    1 8 oz. package cream cheese
    ¼ cup butter
    ½ pound cheddar cheese, grated
    2 tablespoons bleu cheese
    ¼ teaspoon rosemary
    ¼ cup pineapple juice

Let cream cheese and butter warm to room temperature, add cheddar, bleu cheese and seasoning. Add juice, a teaspoonful at a time until all is added. Mix well and chill. Use to stuff celery or spread on slices of raw potato or turnip, or serve as dessert with a plate of apples or winter pears. Makes about 3 cups of spread.

SESAME CHEESE SPREAD

1 cup grated cheese
2 tablespoons salad oil (may use part
    wheat-germ oil here)
2 tablespoons yogurt or home-soured raw cream
1/3 cup ground sesame seed partly toasted
    (see page 36)
1/4 teaspoon each: organic herb seasoning,
    kelp and sea salt
3 tablespoons finely chopped parsley

Blend and use to stuff celery or to top whole-grain toast at breakfast. Makes about 1¼ cups of spread.

TAHINI SPREAD

3/4 cup Tahini (sesame seed butter—obtainable
    at health food stores)
1/2 cup almond, peanut or other nut butter
1/2 cup sunflower seeds or sliced almonds
1 cup currants or raisins, unsulphured
1 teaspoon honey or molasses

Spread on apple or pear slices, or on banana circles. A nutritious meal! Makes 3 cups of spread.

VEGETABLES

VEGETABLES IN SWEET AND SOUR SAUCE

1 tablespoon oil
1/2 cup green pepper, in large dice
1/2 cup celery, sliced
1 apple—in 1/2 inch dice
1 cup pineapple chunks, drained
1/2 cup almonds
Diced cooked chicken or scallops may be used,
    if desired

Stir-fry the vegetables quickly in pan with oil. Add the diced apple, pineapple and almonds and stir-fry again. Add chicken or fish last and cook one minute. Season with 1 teaspoon sea salt. Pour sweet and sour sauce over and serve with steamed brown rice. Garnish with partly toasted sesame seed. Serves 4.

RED SWEET AND SOUR SAUCE

- ¼ cup cider vinegar
- ½ cup pineapple juice
- ½ cup apple juice
- ¼ cup honey
- 2 tablespoons soy sauce
- 1 teaspoon fresh ginger root, chopped or
- 1 tablespoon preserved ginger—chopped
- 2 tablespoons arrowroot
- ¼ cup water
- ¼ cup raw beet juice

Mix vinegar, pineapple and apple juice, honey, soy sauce and ginger. Bring to a boil. Add arrowroot mixed with the water. Cook until clear. Add beet juice.

GREEN PEAS IN SOUR CREAM SAUCE

- 1 cup sour cream or half cream and half yogurt
- ¼ teaspoon organic seasoning
- ¼ teaspoon herbed seasoning
- ½ teaspoon sea salt
- 2 tablespoons finely minced parsley
- 2 mint leaves, chopped, if available

Add any or all of the following:

- 1 green onion, finely sliced
- ¼ cup cucumber, cubed
- ¾ cup sweet red pepper, diced, or sliced radishes
- ¼ cup finely grated carrots

Blend well.

1 package frozen peas, or 2 cups fresh peas. Thaw frozen peas but do not cook. Use fresh peas straight from the pod. When ready to serve, blend prepared sauce gently into peas. Sprinkle top of dish with paprika.

MINTED ZUCCHINI

    3 tablespoons salad oil
    1 medium onion—diced
    2 tablespoons chopped fresh mint
    1 tablespoon fresh sweet basil—chopped
    1 teaspoon fresh sage (or savory or other herb)
    1 teaspoon kelp
    1 teaspoon soy sauce
    2 pounds crisp small zucchini

Slice squash in ½ inch slices. Quickly stir-fry onion and chopped herbs in the oil. Add squash and stir-fry about two minutes. Cover and cook on low for 3 minutes.

Variation: 1 chopped fresh tomato may be added just before serving. Serves 6.

DO-IT-YOURSELF FOODS

HOMEMADE COTTAGE CHEESE

You need 2 quarts of certified raw milk or other milk. Let sit at room temperature until clabbered or "set." Heat very slowly in vessel set inside a kettle filled with hot water (or set inside electric fry pan, with water, on lowest setting) until whey begins to come to the top. Let sit 10 minutes, then drain through a fine sieve or two thicknesses of nylon net lining a colander, or fastened to a small pail with several clean clothes pins. Season with sea salt and, at serving time, add a little cream or "half & half." If you wish to hurry the souring process, add the juice of 4 lemons to the 2 quarts of milk. Stir well, then heat gently and proceed as before.

CALICO COTTAGE CHEESE

    2 cups cottage cheese
    ¼ cup grated carrots
    ¼ cup finely diced green or red sweet peppers
    ¼ cup finely chopped parsley
    ¼ cup shredded radish (omit for younger child)

Mix gently together and serve with a light dusting of paprika on top. 4 servings.

Cottage cheese may be served with a fruit sauce such as apricot or peach purée, blended dried prunes and juice, or sieved berries.

Tomato or avocado slives are delicious when served with creamy cottage cheese.

Fold juice-packed crushed pineapple into cottage cheese for a light luncheon or supper.

HOMEMADE YOGURT

    1 quart milk—**scant** quart
    ¼ cup yogurt for a starter—buy at health
        food store, if possible

Heat the milk in a heavy pan to 115° to 118F°. If you have no thermometer, try a drop on your wrist; it should feel just a little warmer than lukewarm. Stir the yogurt and add a little of the warm milk. Mix until smooth, then stir into the warm milk.

Pour this into a pre-warmed quart jar or into two pint jars. Cover and keep warm (about 115°) for 4 or 5 hours or until thick.

I like to use an insulated picnic box. I fill two quart jars with boiling water and set inside with the empty quart jar in which I culture the yogurt. Then I remove the pre-warmed jar, pour in the yogurt, cover and place in the box again which is by now nicely warm. If the weather is cold, I cover the box with a heavy blanket.

For a thicker yogurt, add ¼ cup dry skim milk powder to the milk before adding yogurt culture. Reserve ¼ cup yogurt for your next starter each time.

YOGURT CHEESE

Place a quart of yogurt in a muslin bag. Tie with a string and hang over your kitchen faucet to drip all night. Catch the whey in a bowl and use for drinks such as lemonade or add to grape juice. The cheese will be a little softer than cream cheese but may be used in most recipes calling for cream cheese.

HOME-SOURED CREAM

2 cups raw certified cream or whipping cream
¼ cup fresh plain yogurt

Place the yogurt in a small bowl and stir until smooth. Slowly add cream and mix well. Let set at room temperature from 12 to 24 hours, until the cream is as firm and sour as you wish. Store in refrigerator until needed.

SPROUTING

HOW TO SPROUT

Use clean, bright new crop seeds—soak overnight 1 tablespoon seeds in 1 quart wide-mouth mason jar. In the morning, drain, saving liquid for soups or broths or green drinks, if palatable, or save for animals to drink. Place the soaked seeds in the jar and cover the top with nylon tulle or stainless steel screen wire, cut to fit. Screw lid on tightly. Water under tap two or three times a day; turn on side in bowl or pan to drain, or set completely upside-down on two small boards or knives to drain well. Grains will be best when the root is as long as the grain. Alfalfa or mung beans can be grown until the sprout is two or three inches long. A little dulse may be added to the soaking water or rinsing water to increase the mineral content of the sprout.

HOW TO USE SPROUTS

Rye or wheat—serve raw with a little honey, raw cream and a sliced fruit for breakfast. Add to soup or salads just before serving. Add to yeast-bread doughs—grind or chop. Work in after all flour is added.

Mung beans and lentils—chop into salads or add to soup at serving time. May be used in oriental dishes or lightly stir-fried for just one or two minutes in a little oil or butter.

Alfalfa, cress or other sprouts—use in green drinks, sandwiches, molded gelatin salads, fruit salad, etc.

TO-MAKE FESTIVE-COLORED FOODS SAFELY

For pink:
Grate raw beet and squeeze in a square of nylon net.
Squeeze pomegranate seeds as above.

For green:
Chop parsley or spinach *very* finely. Squeeze through the nylon net.

For yellow:
Grate raw carrots and squeeze as above.

Tiny bottles with a dropper may be filled with such safe coloring juices and frozen. Remove as needed and keep in the refrigerator. Use to tint whipped cream; add when partially whipped.

For grated coconut:
Add 1 teaspoon or more to each cup coconut in a glass jar with a cap. Shake until all is tinted.

Place plastic bags over your hands to protect from stain while squeezing juices.

References

Food Is Your Best Medicine, Henry G. Beiler, M.D. New York, Random House. 1965—pp 109-112.

Nutrition and Physical Degeneration, Weston A. Price, D.D.S.—Available from the Price-Pottinger Foundation, 2901 Wilshire Blvd., Suite 345, Santa Monica, California 90403.

A Matter of Life: Blueprint for a Healthy Family. W. Coda Martin, M.D. New York. The Devin-Adair Co. 1964.

"Colic: A New Approach to a Common Problem," Roger C. Grady, M.D. *Parents Magazine* July, 1970 p 42.

The Complete Book of Food and Nutrition, J. I. Rodale and Staff, Rodale Press, Inc. Emmaus, Pennsylvania 1961. pp 763-768.

Metabolic Toxemia of Late Pregnancy: A Disease of Malnutrition. Thomas H. Brewer, M.D. Springfield, Illinois, Charles C. Thomas. 1966.

"Don't Curse the Darkness . . . Light a Candle!" Thomas H. Brewer, M.D. *Journal of Applied Nutrition* 20:23, 1968.

Suggested Supplementary Reading List

"Vitamin B During Pregnancy—A Nine Year Study"
John M. Ellis, M.D.

Order reprint N.F.A. Magazine, May, 1971
N.F.A.
P.O. Box 210,
Atlanta, Texas 75551

Nursing your Baby
Karen Pryor—New York: Harper & Row 1963.

Obtain from book store or public library.

The Womanly Art of Breast Feeding
La Leche League International
9616 Minneapolis Ave.
Franklin Park, Illinois 60131

The First Nine Months of Life
Geraldine Lux Flanagan
Order from La Leche League International, address above.

Let's Live Magazine
444 North Larchmont Blvd.
Los Angeles, California 90004

Sources of Supply

If your local health store cannot supply you with ingredients or supplements, write to the following sources:

1—Eugalen Cultured Mother's Milk Powder
   Comfort Products Company
   Box 742
   Soquel, California
   95073
2—V. E. Irons
   R. Rt. 1
   Box 264
   Cottonwood, California
   96022
3—Westpro Labs, Inc.
   12791 Main Street
   Garden Grove, California
   92640
   Write and ask for an order blank or catalogue.
4—Neo-Life Products
   Miriam Spaulding
   1519 Oak Meadow Lane
   South Pasadena, California
   19030
   Ask for information about "Neo-Life" products by mail.

Index of Recipes

COOKBOOKS ON NATURAL HEALTH
. . . To Help You Eat Better for Less!

☐ **ADD A FEW SPROUTS** (Martha H. Oliver)   **$1.50**

☐ **WHOLE GRAIN BAKING SAMPLER**
   (Beatrice Trum Hunter)   **$2.25**

☐ **MRS. APPLEYARD'S KITCHEN** (L.A. Kent)   **$3.50**

☐ **MRS. APPLEYARD'S SUMMER KITCHEN**
   (L.A. Kent & E.K. Gay)   **$3.50**

☐ **MRS. APPLEYARD'S WINTER KITCHEN**
   (L.A. Kent & E.K. Gay)   **$3.50**

☐ **BETTER FOODS FOR BETTER BABIES** (Gena Larson)   **95ᶜ**

☐ **GOOD FOODS THAT GO TOGETHER** (Elinor L. Smith)   **$2.95**

☐ **MEALS AND MENUS FOR ALL SEASONS** (Agnes Toms)   **$1.25**

☐ **NATURAL FOODS BLENDER COOKBOOK**
   (Frieda Nusz)   **$1.25**

☐ **GOLDEN HARVEST PRIZE WINNING RECIPES**
   (ed. by B.T. Hunter)   **$1.25**

☐ **SOYBEANS FOR HEALTH** (Philip Chen)   **$1.25**

☐ **FOOD AND FELLOWSHIP** (Elizabeth S. Pistole)   **95ᶜ**

☐ **MENNONITE COMMUNITY COOKBOOK**
   (Mary Emma Showalter)   **$1.25**

☐ **EAT THE WEEDS** (Ben Charles Harris)   **$1.25**

Buy them at your local health or book store or use this coupon.

Keats Publishing, Inc. (P.O. Box 876), New Canaan, Conn. 06840 75-G
Please send me the books I have checked above. I am enclosing
$____ (add 35ᶜ to cover postage and handling). Send check or
money order—no cash or C.O.D.'s please.

Mr/Mrs/Miss_____

Address _____

City _____ State _____ Zip_____
(Allow three weeks for delivery)   Printed in U.S.A.

COOKBOOKS ON NATURAL HEALTH
. . . To Help You Eat Better for Less!

☐ **ADD A FEW SPROUTS** (Martha H. Oliver)   **$1.50**

☐ **WHOLE GRAIN BAKING SAMPLER**
   (Beatrice Trum Hunter)   **$2.25**

☐ **MRS. APPLEYARD'S KITCHEN** (L.A. Kent)   **$3.50**

☐ **MRS. APPLEYARD'S SUMMER KITCHEN**
   (L.A. Kent & E.K. Gay)   **$3.50**

☐ **MRS. APPLEYARD'S WINTER KITCHEN**
   (L.A. Kent & E.K. Gay)   **$3.50**

☐ **BETTER FOODS FOR BETTER BABIES** (Gena Larson)   **95ᶜ**

☐ **GOOD FOODS THAT GO TOGETHER** (Elinor L. Smith)   **$2.95**

☐ **MEALS AND MENUS FOR ALL SEASONS** (Agnes Toms)   **$1.25**

☐ **NATURAL FOODS BLENDER COOKBOOK**
   (Frieda Nusz)   **$1.25**

☐ **GOLDEN HARVEST PRIZE WINNING RECIPES**
   (ed. by B.T. Hunter)   **$1.25**

☐ **SOYBEANS FOR HEALTH** (Philip Chen)   **$1.25**

☐ **FOOD AND FELLOWSHIP** (Elizabeth S. Pistole)   **95ᶜ**

☐ **MENNONITE COMMUNITY COOKBOOK**
   (Mary Emma Showalter)   **$1.25**

☐ **EAT THE WEEDS** (Ben Charles Harris)   **$1.25**

Buy them at your local health or book store or use this coupon.

Keats Publishing, Inc. (P.O. Box 876), New Canaan, Conn. 06840   75-G
Please send me the books I have checked above. I am enclosing
$_____ (add 35ᶜ to cover postage and handling). Send check or
money order—no cash or C.O.D.'s please.

Mr/Mrs/Miss_____

Address _____

City _____ State _____ Zip_____
    (Allow three weeks for delivery)   Printed in U.S.A.

The Best in Health Books by
LINDA CLARK, BEATRICE TRUM HUNTER and CARLSON WADE

By Linda Clark
- ☐ **Know Your Nutrition**
- ☐ **Cloth $5.95** ☐ **Paperback $3.50**
- ☐ **Face Improvement Through Exercise and Nutrition**   **$1.75**
- ☐ **Be Slim and Healthy**   **$1.50**
- ☐ **Go-Caution-Stop Carbohydrate Computer**   **95ᶜ**
- ☐ **Light on Your Health Problems**   **$1.25**
- ☐ **The Best of Linda Clark**   **$3.50**

By Beatrice Trum Hunter
- ☐ **Whole Grain Baking Sampler**
- ☐ **Cloth $6.95** ☐ **Paperback $2.25**
- ☐ **Food Additives and Your Health**   **$1.25**
- ☐ **Fermented Foods and Beverages**   **$1.25**
- ☐ **Golden Harvest Prize Winning Recipes** (ed. by BTH)   **$1.25**
- ☐ **Food and Your Health** (Anthology ed. by BTH) **$1.25**

By Carlson Wade
- ☐ **Fats, Oils and Cholesterol**   **$1.50**
- ☐ **Vitamins and Other Supplements**   **$1.25**
- ☐ **Hypertension (High Blood Pressure) and Your Diet**   **$1.50**

Buy them at your local health or book store or use this coupon.

Eight Best-Selling Health Books...
How Many Are Helping You Now?

The Saccharine Disease by T.L. Cleave, M.D. "Saccharine" means related to sugar. The illnesses resulting from the taking of sugar or through the digestion of starch in white flour and bread, white rice or other refined carbohydrates— coronary disease, diabetes, ulcers, obesity and bowel disorders. Includes the famous *Diet Health Card for Longer Life*. ☐ Hardcover $7.95. ☐ Quality paperback $4.95.

☐ **Dr. Wilfred E. Shute's Complete Vitamin E Book.** New, up-to-date research on the life-saving vitamin 30,000,000 of us use daily—its proved usefulness for heart patients, and in the treatment of burns, diabetes, skin ailments and circulatory disease. Hardbound $8.95.

☐ **Mental and Elemental Nutrients** by Carl C. Pfeiffer, M.D. A physician's complete guide to good nutrition and health care. More than 400 pages of information about vitamins, trace elements and other nutrients, illness prevention and treatment—with special diet programs and exercise programs. A *Brain Bio Book*. Hardbound $9.95.

Recipe for Survival by Doris Grant. The publishing debut of England's foremost nutritionist, inventor of the famous "Grant loaf." A factual informative guide through the hazardous paths of healthful living and eating today. ☐ Hardcover $6.95. ☐ Quality paperback $3.95.

Know Your Nutrition by Linda Clark. Almost 100,000 copies in print. The basic course in nutrition by its most authoritative research-author. ☐ Hardcover $5.95. ☐ Quality paperback $3.50.

☐ **Yoga . . . The Art of Living** by Renée Taylor. Illustrated with more than 200 action photographs and drawings. The Hunza-yoga way to better health, with recipes, diet programs and exercises. Quality paperback $3.50.

☐ **Vital Facts About Food** by Otto Carqué. The famous blueprint for good health—long out of print—with more than 250 recipes and menus, day-to-day diet suggestions, and complete analyses of 250 foods. Quality paperback $3.50.

Healing Benefits of Acupressure by F.M. Houston, D.C. The book Linda Clark says "could become one of your most precious possessions." Completely illustrated with two-color diagrams on every page showing the body's "nerve centers" which can be effectively reached with the fingers—to heal by contact. ☐ Hardcover $10.00. ☐ Quality paperback $4.95.

Buy them at your local health or book store or use this coupon.

Keats Publishing, Inc. (P.O. Box 876), New Canaan, Conn. 06840   75-B

Please send me the books I have checked above. I am enclosing $____ (add 35¢ to cover postage and handling). Send check or money order—no cash or C.O.D.'s please.

Mr/Mrs/Miss_____

Address _____

City _____ State _____ Zip_____

(Allow three weeks for delivery)